P9-DDD-648

THE
SACRED
ACRE

THE
SACRED
ACRE

The Ed Thomas Story

MARK TABB

with
THE ED THOMAS FAMILY

ZONDERVAN.com/
AUTHORTRACKER
follow your favorite authors

ZONDERVAN

The Sacred Acre
Copyright © 2011 by Parkersburg Productions, LLC

This title is also available as a Zondervan ebook.
Visit www.zondervan.com/ebooks.

This title is also available in a Zondervan audio edition.
Visit www.zondervan.fm.

Requests for information should be addressed to:

Zondervan, *Grand Rapids, Michigan 49530*

Library of Congress Cataloging-in-Publication Data

Tabb, Mark A.
    The sacred acre : the Ed Thomas story / Mark Tabb with the Ed Thomas family.
        p.   cm.
    ISBN 978-0-310-33219-0 (hardcover)
        1. Thomas, Ed, 1950-2009. 2. Christian biography—Iowa—Parkersburg. 3. Murder
victims—Iowa—Parkersburg—Biography. 4. Football coaches—Iowa—Parkersburg—
Biography. 5. Parkersburg (Iowa)—Biography. I. Title.
    BR1725.T454T33   2011
    364.152'3092—dc22   2011015913

Published in association with the literary agency of Alive Communications, Inc., 7680 Goddard Street, Suite 200, Colorado Springs, CO 80920. www.alivecommunications.com

Cover design: *Curt Diepenhorst*
Cover photography: *Matthew Putney*
Cover background: *Shutterstock®*
Interior design: *Beth Shagene*

Printed in the United States of America

11 12 13 14 15 16 17 18 /DCI/ 22 21 20 19 18 17 16 15 14 13 12 11 10 9 8 7 6 5 4 3 2 1

*I want my legacy to be
that I wasn't just a football coach,
but a man who tried to live a Christian life
and impact others.*
ED THOMAS

CONTENTS

FOREWORD
BY TONY DUNGY

I first heard about Coach Ed Thomas in 2005. Our team, the Indianapolis Colts, won its first thirteen games that year and finished 14 and 2, and I was named National Football League Coach of the Year by a number of organizations. That same season, Ed Thomas was named High School Coach of the Year by the NFL. Ed coached at Aplington-Parkersburg High in Parkersburg, Iowa, and over the course of thirty-four years led them to a record of 292 and 84 and two state championships. That is a tremendous accomplishment in itself, but even more remarkable is the fact that from this town of 2,000 people, Ed sent four players to the NFL.

But that's not why Ed Thomas was selected Coach of the Year in 2005. He was selected because of the impact he had on every young man who played for him. Coach Thomas was an inspiration, a role model to each one of them. Not just the ones who would go on to play college or professional football, but to every single boy who played for him. In this small town, one Sacred Acre was dedicated to the raising and building of young men—and not just to be champions on the field. Yes, that was important. But Ed knew that what happens on Friday night is very much related to what happens on the other nights of the week. He aimed to coach the whole player: body, mind, soul, and spirit. And it didn't matter if you were a star player or a third-stringer. Everybody was important. No young man was ever a waste of time.

I believe in those things as well, and I tried to coach the same way. However, I believe that Ed Thomas, doing it at the high school level, had an impact that most professional coaches could never have. A professional coach may get more notoriety, but Coach Thomas didn't just teach the players. He taught the rest of the student body, the faculty and staff, and the parents. He impacted a whole town, and he did it for three generations. In a sport where toughness is valued and coaches are evaluated by their wins and losses, Ed never bought into that value system. Teaching these boys how to become real men was how he always viewed his job.

Ed Thomas was a man who lived the gospel, loved his family, and believed in doing things the right way. He taught his players that there are no shortcuts and that you will ultimately be judged, not by what you did, but on *how* you did it. He was loved, not just by the people of Parkersburg, but by a nation. So when I heard the news on June 24, 2009, that Ed had been tragically taken from us, my reaction was like that of many others. Shock turned to grief in knowing that my profession had lost one of the truly great men to ever step onto a football field. I was honored to be able to place a phone call to his family and express my condolences. Now, as I have gotten to know his wife and children and been able to speak with some of his former players, my admiration for him has deepened even further.

I never had the privilege of meeting Ed Thomas personally, but I felt like I knew him through some of the men who played for him. The Bible says in Matthew 7:16 that a tree is known by its fruit, and through these players, I have seen the fruit of Ed's life. His heart, his faith, and his Christian character are evident in so many of them. He was a master seed planter who worked hard to till the soil of his Sacred Acre. I believe that reading this book will give you a better understanding of this special man and the example he left for all of us to follow.

A NOTE FROM THE ED THOMAS FAMILY

My husband always encouraged his players to "play four quarters!" In other words, to play with heart, with enthusiasm, to never quit, to never stop being your best. You see, football was more than just Xs and Os to Ed. He often said that if all he taught his boys was how to play football, then he would have failed as a coach. "I want them to learn the intangibles that will make them a better husband, dad, member of their community and church." Faith, family, and football. It's on every helmet.

Ed loved the game of football, of course. And he loved his players. And they won more than 80 percent of their games. But that's not why those boys loved Ed; that's not what changed the course of their lives off the field. Ed's greatest legacy was leading by example. A close friend said it best: "True toughness is doing what's right all the time, and Ed was the toughest guy I knew." The core values of his faith—honesty, integrity, respect, honor, doing what is right—these are the life-changing intangibles those boys caught from Ed more than any footballs.

Now, Ed wasn't perfect, and he would be the first to grin a bit sheepishly and agree. But there can be no question that his passion guided those boys, inspired them, showed them the way to become men. "Play four quarters," Ed would scream over the din of the crowd, and those boys would hear it and give it all they had. That's leadership—not for glory, not for self, but for love of another who gave his all for them.

Ed didn't draw attention to himself, and he would be embarrassed to see that a book has been written about him. But my sons and I hope that by sharing this humble man's story, you will be inspired to find your own passion

to use the gifts that God has given you,

to do what's right,

to lead by example.

And then to get out there and "play all four quarters!" Ed is counting on you. So are your kids, your spouse, the people you work with.

We miss you, Ed. The boys are good. You left an example to follow.

All our love,

Jan Thomas

Todd Thomas

Aaron Thomas

THE SACRED ACRE

Take care of the little things,
and the big things will take care of themselves.
ED THOMAS

EVERYONE IN PARKERSBURG AND BEYOND REFERRED TO THE home football field of Aplington-Parkersburg High School as "the Sacred Acre"—everyone, that is, except the team's head coach. Ed Thomas referred to it as "the field where my team plays." While technically correct, his perspective doesn't tell the whole story. The A-P Falcons played on the field next to the high school, a field flanked on either side by metal bleachers like those you will find at any small high school anywhere in the country, especially in the Midwest. And *only* the A-P Falcon football team played on the field next to the school. The football field may have been school property, but the school didn't get to use it. No one but the football team was allowed to set foot on it. Coach Thomas let the band perform their halftime shows on the field, but he did not let them practice on it during the week. Nor did he let A-P's gym classes play soccer or rugby or even tag on the field. In the spring, when the track team used the track that circled the field, Ed roped off the football playing surface to keep sprinters and distance runners from stretching or warming up inside the white lines where only the football team was allowed to stretch and warm up. Only on the rarest of occasions did he let his team practice on their home field through the week. Practice was held on the field on the opposite side of Johnson Street, across from the high school.

If Ed seemed a little obsessive about his football field, there was a good reason for it. He was a lot obsessive about his football field. He took better care of it than his own lawn. On the few occasions when his wife, Jan, could talk him into mowing the yard, he shot around it with the mower like a teenage boy listening to heavy metal music surrounded by pretty girls. He missed wide patches of grass on one side of the house and scalped it down to dirt on the other. When he finished, Jan would walk outside and shake her head. "Really, Ed," she would say, "that's the best you can do?"

"What?" he said with that little smirk of his that always put a smile on Jan's face. "It looks good enough to me."

"If that's the case, then I better make you an appointment with the eye doctor," Jan quipped.

"Well, a couple of spots may not look so great, but that's because the lawn mower blade is dull. I'll take care of that later."

"Yeah, right," Jan said, amused. The thought of her husband sharpening the blade on their lawn mower struck her as absurd. Ed Thomas was many things, but handy was not one of them.

As soon as Ed left the house, Jan went outside and redid the lawn herself to make it less of an eyesore.

The football field was another story entirely. Ed meticulously went over it like Michelangelo putting the finishing touches on the statue of David. From early spring to late fall Ed mowed it twice a week ("to promote growth," he said), making sure to mow in the same direction between the yard lines. That way the grass had the distinctive contrasting shades of green every five yards, like the college and professional fields. He also watered and fertilized and aerated and overseeded and applied weed killers and bug killers, whether the field needed them or not. When it rained, he drove over to make sure the water drained properly, and in the hot summer months when rain rarely fell, he set out sprinklers and watered it himself until the school finally installed an irrigation system. All in all, he babied the field as if it sat in the middle of the University of Iowa's Kinnick Stadium, not between metal bleachers in the middle of a small town in northeast Iowa. Most people said that the field at Kinnick Stadium was the only field in the state of Iowa that compared to A-P's. The university employed a staff of professional groundskeepers; A-P only had Ed Thomas, but that was enough.

Ed's passion for the field where his team played football started at an early age. Long before Parkersburg High School hired him to coach and teach government and economics, back when Ed was in junior high school, he pulled the neighborhood kids together to play pickup football games in the large yard in front of his grandmother's house. This was no ordinary yard. He found a couple of bags of lime that he used to mark off yard lines and end zones. It only seemed natural for him to keep right on caring for his field himself when he became a football coach right out of college.

When Ed arrived in Parkersburg in 1975 after three years at Northeast Hamilton High School in Blairsburg, Iowa, he immediately took ownership of the field. He mowed it during the off-season, and sprayed the weeds that sprung up in the gravel separating the field from the running track. Before long he found himself attacking the weeds that grew up around the forty yard line. That's when he noticed the grass wasn't quite as green as he wanted it to be, which led to a round of fertilizer applied to the field himself. And then he said the yard lines weren't chalked off to his liking, so he started doing that himself, along with putting down the numbers.

Sometime in the late 1970s or 80s, Ed found a secondhand watering system that he bought with his own money—an odd menagerie of copper pipes that had to be manually connected to a fire hydrant on the edge of the high school parking lot. The pipes only covered half of the field, which meant Ed had to come back at a later time and move them from one end to the other. The job was too big for one man to do by himself, so Ed enlisted Jan to help.

When their two sons were big enough to lift and carry the pipes, they took their mother's place.

Ed was the kind of guy who had a schedule for everything connected with his football program, and watering the field was no different. Nothing got in the way of his timetable, not even his own absence. Not long after he purchased the secondhand watering system, he and one of his assistant coaches, Al Kerns, had to go to a coaching clinic in Cedar Falls. Ed called one of his buddies, Jim Graves, and asked him to take care of the field for him. "I'll start the water before I leave," Ed told him, "but I'll need you to come over and turn it off for me at 10:30 p.m. sharp. I'll leave a key to the fire hydrant for you at my house."

"Sure, Ed," Jim said, "I'll take care of it."

A little before 10:30, Jim walked out to his car to head over to the field. He could see the high school parking lot from his house, and he noticed a police car and a city water department truck already there. Jim rushed over, parked his pickup truck, and walked over to the fire hydrant off to the side of the field. "Hey, guys," he said to the policeman and the city worker standing next to the hydrant, "is there a problem?"

The city worker looked up. "The low pressure alarm went off on the water tower. I traced the problem to the field here. I need to shut the sprinklers off, but the hydrant is locked and I don't have a key. Do you know what the coach did with it?"

"I've got the key in my truck," Jim said.

The policeman and city worker looked at each other and smiled as if to say, "Great. Finally." "So will you shut it off for us?" the policeman asked.

Jim glanced at his watch. "Well, Coach told me not to shut it off until 10:30, and it ain't 10:30 yet."

"OK, we can wait," the policeman said without arguing the point. A few minutes later Jim turned the water off — at precisely 10:30.

Later that night, when Ed returned home, Jim called and said,

"I want you to know that there were a lot of people in town taking showers tonight who didn't get rinsed off because your Sacred Acre needed water." Ed laughed, but for Jim, the name stuck.

Jim and Ed and several other locals got together most mornings to drink coffee at the local feed store. One morning, Ed talked Jim into replacing the lights on the football field. Jim worked for the local power company. When it came to Ed Thomas, it didn't take much persuasion to talk Jim into it. "Sure," he told Ed, "whatever you need."

"Now when you get out there with your equipment and start digging holes for the new poles, make sure you keep them away from the field. That kind of equipment can put ruts in the turf, you know," Ed said to Jim.

"Yeah, I know."

"And when you cut the trench between the poles to bury the electrical lines, make sure you keep the trencher off the field. I don't want anyone trampling down the grass."

"Don't worry, Ed. I won't touch your Sacred Acre." The rest of the guys in the group howled with laughter.

After that, the name spread. Every morning, someone managed to make some sort of comment about Ed's Sacred Acre. One day it was Delbert Huisman—everyone called him Stub—who said, "Hey, Eddie. Drove by your Sacred Acre today. I could have sworn I saw a dandelion popping up around the fifty yard line. You better get out there and pull it up. You know how dandelions spread." Another day it was Willie Vanderholt, who owned the local feed store where they met for coffee, who chimed in, "I heard there were some kids out last night running up and down your Sacred Acre. You better check to make sure the lock is still on the gate." Everyone laughed and laughed with each comment, including Ed. However, after they finished their coffee, Ed went down to the high school and took a look around his field to make sure no dandelions had invaded and that the lock was still firmly in place on the gate. More than once, he discovered dandelions spread out across the field. They hadn't grown up overnight. His coffee-drinking buddies had put them there as a joke.

Ed never minded his friends' razzing because he knew his obsession with the field was not about a 360- by 160-foot plot of grass. His Sacred Acre served as a symbol of a much larger lesson he wanted to convey to the young men who signed up to play football for him. Prior to his arrival, Parkersburg High School had only fielded three winning teams since it started football in 1958. In thirty-four seasons under Ed Thomas, they only had one losing season. Along the way, Ed compiled 292 victories, along with two state championships, four state runners-up, and nineteen play-off appearances. Every season, Ed preached the same life lessons of hard work, focus, commitment, and attention to the smallest detail. "If we do the little things right," he told his teams, "the big things will take care of themselves." One glance over at the football field made it clear that Coach Thomas practiced what he preached.

The A-P football field also showed one of Ed's greatest gifts, a gift that endeared him to people in a way not even he fully understood. Back when Parkersburg High School (before the consolidation with Aplington) was built in 1970, athletic fields were an afterthought. Bulldozers moved dirt from the north side of the building site to level the pad where the school was built, leaving behind a flat spot that consisted of rock and hard clay. Later they brought in some topsoil, spread it on top of that flat spot, and declared it the football field. Getting any kind of grass to grow on the hard clay had never been easy. But Ed was not going to settle for merely getting grass to grow. He wanted an exceptional field, and he saw no reason why this patch of clay and rock couldn't be just that. He saw potential in a throwaway plot of ground that no one else could see. Through the years, he coaxed more out of that ground than anyone ever thought possible. He did the same thing with every player who came out for his team.

After the final home game of the 2007 season, Ed did something that made most people in town think he had lost his mind. He lowered the mowing deck on his riding mower and scalped his football field down to the dirt. Then he covered the field with a thick layer of sand. He spread seed over the sand and covered the entire field with a tarp for the winter. His wife couldn't believe her eyes. "Why would you do that?" she asked several times. "The field looked so nice already." Ed just smiled and told her to trust him. He hadn't lost his mind. An agricultural professor from Iowa State University gave him the idea and told him how to carry it out. What others saw as desecration, Ed saw as a necessary step toward an even better field.

When spring rolled around and he removed the tarp from the field, Ed proved the doubters wrong. Not only did the field look better than ever; it drained water more efficiently and recovered faster from the wear and tear of the football season. Once again, this was about more than a football field. Ed's efforts told his team and the rest of the community never to rest on past successes but to always push themselves to improve every day, no matter what that day might hold. To Ed, bad days said more about a person's character than the good, and to him, nothing mattered more than character.

No, Ed never cared for the name Sacred Acre, but everyone else in town loved it. To Parkersburg and Aplington, the field and the man who gave it such meticulous care were inseparable. Everyone held the field in such esteem because they had such respect for Ed Thomas. For Ed Thomas and the players and their families he touched during his thirty-four years in Parkersburg, the field was about more than a field, and the game was about more than a game.

In *The Imitation of Christ*, Thomas à Kempis wrote, "It is vanity to wish for long life and to care little about a well-spent life." Though unexpectedly cut short, Ed Thomas's life was well spent. When he first arrived in Parkersburg, he saw the school as the next step in his coaching career, not a final destination. Like most young coaches, he dreamed of ascending the ranks to larger schools in bigger cities, perhaps even moving on to the college ranks. Somewhere along the way, he figured out that his mission lay not in wins and losses but in making his players more successful in life. For Ed, the best place to do just that was as head football coach of the Aplington-Parkersburg Falcons on a field everyone but he called the Sacred Acre.

CHAPTER 1

EF5

When the wind starts blowing,
don't tell me about the hurricane;
just bring the ship home, fellas.
ED THOMAS

A LOW RUMBLE OF THUNDER RATTLED THE GLASS IN THE windows of Ed Thomas's classroom. He glanced outside and noticed the sky had grown much darker since he arrived at the school a few minutes earlier. "Looks like the farmers at church this morning were on the money," he said to himself. "They said we were going to get a storm today and, by golly, they're right." He turned back to his desk and pulled a key out of the top drawer. One of his upcoming senior football players had asked for a key to the weight room so he could work out the next day. Any other Monday morning, Ed would have opened the weight room himself, usually by 6:00 a.m. Since tomorrow was Memorial Day, he had other plans. Of course, Ed was more than happy to give a key to any player who wanted to push himself. The very thought of it put a smile on his lips. That was the kind of dedication and leadership he wanted from his seniors.

The loud blast of the tornado siren broke Ed's train of thought. He had never heard it so loud in his second home, Aplington-Parkersburg High School on the south side of Parkersburg, Iowa.

For years, the only tornado siren in town sat on the north side. The wind had to be just right for people on the south side to hear it. All that had changed two days earlier, when city workers installed a brand-new siren near the high school. They installed it on Friday, tested it on Saturday, and now set it off for the first time at 4:46 p.m., Sunday, May 25, 2008.

Ed grabbed a handful of copies of "2007 Aplington-Parkersburg Football" DVDs, which he gave as gifts to all graduating seniors, and then walked calmly out of his room and down the hall. The siren didn't add any sense of urgency. Half an hour earlier, while leaving a graduation party at a local restaurant in the nearby town of Aplington, he had talked to a couple of firemen who were on their way out the door as weather spotters. Both seemed more concerned about Ed's opinion about his team's prospects for the next football season than they were about the storm clouds growing in the west.

Scattered raindrops hit Ed as he walked outside. It wasn't much, but from the looks of the western sky, he knew the heavy stuff wasn't far behind. "I better go get my golf cart before this thing hits," he said. He'd spent the first part of the afternoon playing golf with his youngest son, Todd, and Todd's soon to be father-in-law, Mike Brannon. Ed had to take off after nine holes to attend the numerous high school graduation parties going on that afternoon and evening. Rather than use one of the rental carts from the golf course, Ed had his own. It was his most treasured possession. A few years earlier, the community and his players, past and present, presented it to him when he won his two hundredth game as a coach. He even had a special trailer for it, which he pulled behind his pickup truck. Before he left the afternoon golf game, Ed told Todd to leave the cart at the course, and he would pick it up later. This was later enough.

Ed climbed in his car and drove the three blocks from the school to his house on the far south side of Parkersburg. As he walked in the front door, he called out to his wife. "Hey, Jan, where are you?"

"I'm in the basement where more people should be. You need to get down here, NOW!" she said. Ed and Jan put in the basement during the first of the three home additions they had made over the course of ten years. When they bought the house a year after they married, it was quite small, just over eight hundred square feet. As their budget and family grew in size, they added on to it—first another bedroom, then a new kitchen, and finally a new living room and bathroom. They added the basement with the bedroom. Since Iowa is known for tornadoes, it seemed like the thing to do. However, Ed never expected to have to use it. Legend had it that a tornado could not strike Parkersburg because it sat at the fork of a river. Up until Memorial Day weekend, 2008, the legend seemed pretty accurate.

"I need to go get my golf cart first. I'll be right back."

"Forget the golf cart," Jan said. "Channel 7 said this storm is really bad. I heard the fire trucks go by on their way out of town right after the storm sirens went off. That can't be good, not if they're moving fire trucks out of harm's way."

"Oh, it can't be that bad. The television always blows these things way out of proportion. I don't want to leave my golf cart out in the rain. I'll be right back."

"No! There isn't any time."

"I looked around when I came home. I didn't see anything."

"You couldn't see anything because of all the trees. Grab your pillow and get down here fast." A trained emergency medical technician (EMT) and volunteer first responder with the local ambulance service, Jan knew that most injuries in storms come from flying debris. That's why she knew to take her pillow with her to the basement when the storm sirens went off.

"All right, you win," Ed said. Thirty-two years of marriage had taught him that some arguments are best lost. He went into their bedroom, grabbed his pillow off his bed, and walked down into the basement, closing the door behind him.

Ed found Jan under the basement stairs, but he didn't join

her there. He stood in the middle of the basement floor, his arms crossed, with a look on his face that said, "I'm here. Are you happy now?" No sooner had he crossed his arms than they heard a loud rush of wind, like the dry cycle of the car wash on steroids.

"Do you hear that!?" Jan said.

"Yeah," Ed said. He dropped his arms, grabbed his pillow, and jumped under the basement steps with Jan. Both of them barely fit in the space under the stairs. The two curled up into a near-fetal position next to one another, their faces less than an inch apart, their arms holding their pillows tightly against their heads. Above their heads, a freight train plowed into their house. Boards snapped. Glass shattered. A deafening cracking sound started at one end of the house and raced toward the other.

Ed and Jan looked at each other, their eyes wide with fear. They both started praying out loud, their voices drowned out by the wind that grew louder and louder. Dirt dropped down on top of the two of them. Jan peeked out once and saw nothing but absolute black. "Oh, God, please don't let the house collapse on top of us!" she cried out.

"AMEN!" Ed said.

And then, as quickly as it started, the wind stopped. Everything grew still and silent. "I'm going out there," Ed said.

"No, wait just a minute. There could still be more," Jan said.

"I really think it is over. I want to go up and have a look around, make sure everything is OK."

Ed was the optimist of the family, Jan the realist. She looked him in the eye and said, "You know when you open that door that our house is gone, don't you?"

"You think?" Ed said in a doubtful tone.

"Absolutely. It's gone."

◆ ◆ ◆

Two houses down the block, Todd Thomas and Candice, his fiancée, were at the home of Mike and Nancy Brannon, Candice's parents. Candice and Nancy spent most of the afternoon working on the wedding invitations, along with Jan. Jan left when the television weatherman warned of an approaching storm. Todd and Mike played golf with Ed. They played only three additional holes after Ed left to head for the graduation parties. A clubhouse attendant came out to the thirteenth tee box and said, "A big storm is heading our way. You need to clear the course." Todd didn't want to leave. He was up by several strokes and hated to waste a good game of golf. But playing in the rain wasn't exactly his idea of a good time, so they did as they were told. The tornado siren went off not long after Todd and Mike made it back to Mike's house. As soon as the siren started blaring, Candice and Nancy darted for the basement. Todd and Mike headed toward the front door.

"Where are you going?" Candice asked.

"To take a look," Todd said.

"A look? At what?" Candice said.

"You know, the storm, to see if anything is headed our way," Todd said in a matter-of-fact "duh, what else do you do when tornado sirens go off?" tone. "We won't be out there a minute. I promise."

Candice rolled her eyes and ran downstairs. Todd and Mike walked out into the front yard. The wind and rain that chased them off the golf course earlier had stopped, replaced by a dead calm. Silence hung in the air. Nothing made a sound. No dogs barked in the distance; no bird sang, and not even an insect buzzed. Parkersburg felt and sounded abandoned.

"Wow, that's weird," Todd said.

"Yeah, I've never felt anything quite like this before," Mike replied.

"Get ready. I've got a feeling something is about to happen," Todd said.

The two of them looked out toward the west. Storms in Iowa always travel west to east. A huge black cloud covered the western sky, and it appeared to be moving closer. A strong breeze suddenly hit Todd in the face. The cloud climbed over the hill on the far side of town, moving closer to the lumberyard a quarter mile from Mike's home. Suddenly, the lumberyard exploded as the cloud fell on top of it. Sheet metal and two-by-fours and poles flew through the air.*

"Crap, let's get outta here!" Todd shouted. They ran into the house, flew down the stairs of the basement, and dove under the pool table, where Candice and Nancy were huddled. Only then did they hear the proverbial freight train sound. Todd couldn't quite fit his six-foot-five frame under the pool table. His legs stuck out exposed.

Glass crashed overhead, followed by a loud tumbling, rolling sound. "I think that was the couch," Mike said.

Nancy turned on a flashlight and prayed. "It's going to be all right," Todd said to Candice as he held her hand. He felt debris dropping onto his legs. "Please God, don't let anything heavy come down on top of me!" he prayed aloud.

Boards cracked and snapped. The smell of fresh lumber filled the basement. "And there goes the roof," Mike said. Nancy prayed harder.

The moment the noise stopped, Todd jumped up and headed toward the stairs. "I've got to check on my mom and dad," he said.

"Todd, expect the worst," Mike said.

Todd nodded and ran upstairs. Most of the roof and walls of the house were gone. "What the ...?" he said when he looked at the dining room table. It had not moved, and neither had the stack of wedding invitations on top of it. He glanced over to where he had parked his 2006 Nissan Maxima. A tree had sliced the car in half.

Todd ran out into the Brannon's front yard. He could not believe his eyes. Every house, every business, for as far as he could see, had been reduced to piles of rubble.† He looked around from side to

*For raw footage of the tornado striking Parkersburg, go to *www.youtube.com/watch?v=lAPnbzHvIKs&feature=fvsr*.
†For on-the-scene news coverage of the aftermath of the tornado, go to *www.youtube.com/watch?v=lueETqSXcKo&feature=fvw*.

side. A few minutes earlier, the town sounded abandoned; now it looked completely deserted. "Where is everybody?" he said. "Oh, my gosh, didn't anyone else survive?"

He had been told to "expect the worst," but this was worse than his mind could imagine. Almost worse. Where were his parents? Were they OK? His mother had called him right before the storm hit, asking if he knew where his father was. If Todd knew his dad, and he did, then he was probably down at the golf course loading up his golf cart right when the tornado blew through town. "And if Dad was there, then ..." Todd pushed those thoughts out of his head. "Mom! Dad! Are you OK?" he shouted as he ran toward his parents' house.

Todd jumped over a set of downed power lines and ran the short distance from the Brannons' home to his parents' home. "Mom! Dad!" he yelled as he ran into their yard. The storm had thrown a flatbed trailer into the side of Ed and Jan's house where the front door had once been. It held up what little of their roof remained. "How am I going to get in?" Todd said before he realized that all of the walls of the house were gone with the lone exception of one interior wall with the door to the basement. "MOM! DAD!" he shouted.

"We're fine. We're down here," he heard his father yell. Todd flung open the basement door and ran down the stairs. He threw his arms around both of them.

"We're OK," his mother said in a matter-of-fact tone. Ed, the rough-and-tumble football coach, choked back tears. Not Jan. Nothing ever seemed to faze her. "Go check on Marian," she said. Marian DeBoer was their retired, widowed neighbor who lived by herself. Jan had tried to get her to come over and join her in the Thomas basement before the storm. She refused, saying she would be fine in her own basement.

Ed followed Todd up the stairs. He glanced back at Jan, who seemed to lag behind. "Are you coming?" he asked.

"Yes, but of all the dumb things to do," she said.

"What?"

"I was so intent on getting down here when the sirens went off that I forgot my shoes. I grabbed my pillow and completely forgot my shoes."

"Do you want me to help you find some?"

"No, go and check on the neighbors. I'll be all right."

Ed did as he was told, and as he climbed out of the basement, he found himself out in the open, even while inside what had been his living room a couple of minutes earlier. Upended cars littered the streets around him. Shattered boards stood where houses had once been. "It looks like a war zone," he said to Todd. Ed turned toward his bedroom, or at least where his bedroom was supposed to be. The rest of his house, along with the entire neighborhood, was gone. The large maple trees that lined the streets had all been stripped bare and mangled into deformed skeletons.

He turned and walked in the general direction of where the front door used to be. "What on earth?" he said at the sight of the flatbed trailer wedged into his house. Off to one side he saw his pickup truck. It looked like someone had taken a giant can opener to it. The golf cart trailer was nowhere to be seen.

Looking past his truck, he stared off to the north and east, toward his second home, A-P High School. Even from a half mile away, he could see that the top half of the gym was gone. He couldn't tell how badly damaged the rest of the buildings might be, but even from this distance he knew it wasn't good. His head spun as his mind tried to process what his eyes saw. Ed leaned over with his hands on his knees as if he had just been punched in the stomach. In a way, he had.

Jan emerged from the basement and came up behind him. She glanced around quickly. "Wow. I knew it would be bad, but this is worse than I imagined."

"This is just unbelievable," Ed said, his voice cracking.

Behind them, a loud scream pierced their ears. Ed and Jan turned and saw one of Ed's students, a seventeen-year-old girl, in hysterics. Todd had just returned from helping Marian out of her basement. She had come through the storm unharmed, but her house was gone. "Todd!" Jan yelled.

"I'm on it," he said and took off running toward the screaming girl. Ed followed behind.

"Where are my shoes?" Jan said as she dug around through the rubble that had been their bedroom five minutes earlier. "Ha, found one," she said, pulling a soaked canvas tennis shoe out from under a pile of wet Sheetrock. She dug around some more, frustrated. Finally, she found the match. Not only were both shoes soaked; dirt and fiberglass insulation filled the insides. Jan dumped out as much of the crud as she could and slid them on. They were better than no shoes at all.

Todd ran back over. The frantic girl was screaming because her neighbor, an older man who was like a grandfather to her, had been badly injured when his house collapsed into the basement. "Mom, you need to get over here quickly. Chuck is hurt pretty bad."

"OK," Jan said. As soon as she reached him, she knew Charles Horan was in trouble. Blood gushed from a gash in his head. Lifting his shirt, she saw severe blunt force trauma injuries across his chest. "I've got to get the ambulance. Stay here. I'll send help," she said.

Todd and Ed stayed with Chuck as Jan took off running toward the fire station. She hoped the station would still be there when she arrived. As soon as she was gone, Todd looked at his father. "How many others do you think are hurt like this?" he asked.

Ed looked around at what remained of the south side of Parkersburg. It looked like old black-and-white photos of Hiroshima after the atomic bomb had decimated the city, albeit on a much, much smaller scale. He let out a long sigh. "I'm afraid to even guess," he said.

Rain began to fall again. The rainstorm the farmers predicted had finally arrived.

CHAPTER 2

NO PLACE
LIKE HOME

Never forget where you came from.
ED THOMAS

ED DIDN'T GROW UP IN PARKERSBURG, BUT YOU COULDN'T tell it from talking to him. He spoke of the small town of 1,900 in northeast Iowa as second only to the garden of Eden itself. If you didn't know better, you would have thought he was president of the local Chamber of Commerce rather than the high school football coach. Everywhere he went Ed sang Parkersburg's praises. "Someday," he often said, "the word is going to get out about this place." He never counted on the word getting out quite like this.

A team of storm chasers working with Des Moines television station KCCI pulled into town at 5:03 p.m., less than five minutes after the tornado moved on to the east. They came in on Highway 57, which passes just to the north of the Thomas home. Immediately, the storm chasers called into their contact at the station. "We have pretty much impassable roads out here, massive damage, houses completely obliterated, leaking gas here," one member of the team said. "I need you to do something for public safety. We have huge gas leaks. I need to have emergency management send everybody they have here. Firefighters. State police. Everyone.

We're talking massive destruction. Large gas leaks. We have possible lots of fatalities. Cars flipped. This is not good." The storm chasers tried to jump into rescue mode, but the air reeked of natural gas, forcing them out of town in fear of sparking a fire.*

KCCI Channel 8 immediately broadcast their report from Parkersburg. Other television and radio stations across the state repeated it. Wire services all over the country soon picked up the story. Details were still sketchy, but one thing seemed clear: some, if not all, of Parkersburg had been destroyed.

Five miles straight west of town, Ellie Thomas sat glued to the television. The birthday party she had attended that afternoon came to a screeching halt due to the storms rolling across northeast Iowa. As soon as she heard the initial reports coming out of Parkersburg, she grabbed her cell phone and called her husband, Aaron, Ed and Jan's oldest son.

"Aaron, where are you right now?" Ellie asked.

"I'm still in Dysart at the graduation party. Why? Is the birthday party at your brother's house over already?"

"Haven't you heard the news?" Ellie's voice broke. Try as she might to project a brave front to her husband, her emotions broke through. "A tornado just hit Parkersburg. They say it's real bad."

"OK, that just means some farmer's barn out in the country blew away. Happens every spring. It's not a big deal," Aaron said. Ellie calls Aaron E.J., as in Ed Junior, because he looks and acts so much like his father. Yet, in times of crisis, his mother comes out in him—calm, practical, to the point. That's why news of a tornado hitting his hometown didn't throw him into a panic. Growing up in Iowa, he had lived through many a storm. A downed barn or a lost mobile home constituted a weather catastrophe in Parkersburg. To Aaron, it wasn't anything to get too worked up over.

"No, you don't understand. They just came on the news and reported that a large part of town is completely destroyed. Aaron, I

---

*Watch raw, unedited footage at *www.youtube.com/watch?v=TLx7Xe6_cxo*.

can't get ahold of your folks." Panic filled Ellie's voice. "I'm scared. The people on the news said the storm could be an EF5, the worst there is, and it went right over your parents' house."

"I'm sure they're OK," Aaron said, trying to calm his wife down. His words were as much a prayer as a statement. "Phone service and electricity are probably out. That's why you can't reach them. I'll leave the graduation party right now and drive over and check everything out."

"Please do. And be careful."

"Don't worry. Stay where you are. I'll call you as soon as I know something."

"OK," Ellie said.

Aaron clicked "end" on his cell phone, then turned to his assistant coach, whose son was celebrating his graduation. Like his father, Aaron always wanted to coach, although he preferred basketball to football. He had been a starter on the Division I basketball team at Drake University and then moved right into coaching as a graduate assistant at St. Cloud State University in St. Cloud, Minnesota, after graduating from Drake. One year later, he took over as head basketball coach and athletic director at Union High School in La Porte, Iowa. In his four seasons, he had already started establishing the same reputation as a basketball coach that his father had in football.

"I gotta go," Aaron said to his friend, knowing he had an hour's drive ahead of him. "A tornado just hit Parkersburg. I'm going to drive over and make sure my parents are all right."

"Yeah, uh, OK," his friend said, his mind trying to grasp what he'd just been told. "Let me know what you find out."

"Sure. Not a problem," Aaron said as he headed for the door.

Fifty miles away in Parkersburg, Ed tried to wrap his head around what lay around him. Chuck had been transported to the hospital, but Ed knew he probably wouldn't survive. Ed and Todd had spent what felt like a very long time helping pull neighbors out of basements. Police officers and firefighters converged on the town, but they were badly undermanned in comparison to the level of destruction.

"I've gotta get to the school," Ed said to Todd once all their neighbors were accounted for.

"I'll go with you," Todd said. He was nearly as anxious to get to the school as his father was. Growing up, he had spent nearly as much time at A-P as he had at his home, maybe even more. It was *the* place where he and his father built a special bond. At the age of seven or eight, Todd started out as the ball boy. He and Aaron hung out at practice and ran special errands for their dad. They didn't just tag along after their father. Ed made them feel like they belonged, as if running out on the field to pick up the kicking tee after the kickoff was one of the most important jobs anyone could have. Todd and Aaron also helped sort through the team equipment with their dad and mark off the lines on the practice field, just the three of them. Whenever Ed mowed the football field, Todd and Aaron took turns riding on the mower with him. When Todd was thirteen, his dad even handed him the keys to the riding mower and said, "Why don't you mow the field for me today? I think you can handle it." That was Todd's coming-of-age moment.

Todd and Aaron also had the unenviable task of helping their dad drag the irrigation pipes from one side of the field to the other —doing so from the time they were just big enough to pick the pipes up. Ed usually rewarded them on hot summer days by letting them run through the sprinklers as they watered the field. However, he always made them take off their shoes first. Todd never knew if his dad did that so they would keep their shoes dry, or to protect the grass on the field. Once he was old enough to think it through, he decided it was the latter. Afterward, Ed took his sons into the teacher's lounge and bought them a bottle of pop from the soda machine. Todd never forgot how cold that strawberry pop tasted out of a real glass bottle, or how much fun he had sitting out on the grass, drinking it down, talking and joking with his dad.

The day of the tornado, the three blocks from his house to the high school never seemed longer. Every few steps, Ed and Todd stopped to check on friends and neighbors, and in Parkersburg, everyone was a friend or neighbor to Ed Thomas. In his years as head football coach and history and economics teacher, he had coached or taught at least one member of nearly every family in town. Even with an enrollment that fluctuated between 220 and 250 students from year to year, Ed regularly had 80, 90, even 100 boys come out for football every season. Whenever a local family had a baby boy, Ed sent the parents a certificate that read, "Congratulations! Upon the recommendation of the Aplington-Parkersburg football staff, your newborn son has been officially drafted to become a Falcon football player in the fall of _____." Former players who moved away after high school moved back to town after they settled down and had sons of their own. They returned for one simple reason: they wanted Coach Thomas to impact their sons in the same way he had impacted them.

Parkersburg hadn't always been so crazy about football. Prior to Ed's arrival, girls' basketball was the biggest game in town. Boys played football only to get in shape for basketball season. No one expected much out of the football team — not even the players. Every year they finished near the bottom of their conference. Few people in 1975 thought a new coach could change that. After all, at that time Ed Thomas and Parkersburg had one thing in common: both had trouble winning football games. Ed's first team at Northeast Hamilton High School lost every game they played. The next year he managed to win two but lost seven. His third team was his first to win more than it lost, finishing the year five and four. That also happened to be the year Ed started dating Jan. She never tired of pointing out to him that he never had a winning record until he met her. Even so, his 7 and 20 overall record didn't elicit great confidence in him as a football coach. Ed, however, never once doubted his abilities.

Twenty boys came out for football in Ed's first season at Parkersburg High School. Halfway through the first practice, senior captain Dave Becker knew this season would be unlike anything he had ever experienced before. He looked around at the twenty other guys on the team, their heads hanging down, exhausted. Most of them expected Coach Thomas to blow the whistle at any moment and tell them to hit the showers and head home. Practice had already lasted longer than their previous coach's practices. Then Dave looked over at Ed. "OK, fellas," Ed yelled out, "get over here and line up. We've got a lot of work yet to do. Remember, all the hard work we put in out here on the practice field will pay off on Friday nights."

A couple of guys near Dave groaned. Not Dave. He had been waiting for a coach who not only wanted to win but believed this group of twenty farm boys could pull it off. "All right, you guys, you heard the coach. Line up," Dave yelled. The other seniors hit the line first, and the underclassmen followed.

Ed looked over at Dave and gave him a little smile.

"Coach, we're sick of getting our butts handed to us every game," Dave said.

"I'll tell you what, Becker, if you fellas will work hard and work together, I guarantee you that the sky is the limit on what we can accomplish here. We may not be as talented as some of the teams we're going to play this season, but, by golly, we're going to beat them by outworking them."

"I'm with you," Dave said. "Let's do this."

Ed slapped him on the back. "All right, get down in your stance. Fire off the line on the whistle."

Parkersburg won their first game of the season, followed by another three wins in a row. When they finally lost a game, Ed didn't yell at the players for their mistakes. In the locker room he told them how proud he was of their effort and asked them one question: "What did you learn from the mistakes we made out there tonight?" The team finished the year with six wins and only three losses. It was Parkersburg's first winning season in over twenty years. Ed bought shirts for every young man on the team, with "6–3" across the front, and the words "A Tradition Is Born" on the back.

Ed didn't set out to simply change the culture within the team; he set out to change the culture throughout the school and the entire community. Joan Prohaska decided to go out for the cheerleading squad during Ed's second season, her senior year. She assumed all she had to do was to make it through the tryouts. Then Ed called all the prospective cheerleaders into his classroom for a meeting. "Please have a seat, ladies," he said. He then passed out a test they had to pass before they were allowed on the sidelines of Ed's football field—a test of their basic knowledge of the game of football. He didn't want anyone leading cheers for his team if they didn't know the difference between a first down and an incomplete pass.

Dave Becker and Joan started dating and later got married after she graduated from high school. They moved away from Parkersburg, but not for long. They moved back to town after starting a family of their own. Dave wanted his children to be around Ed in the hope that some of Coach would rub off on them and influence their lives in the same way he had influenced his. Eventually, all three of their sons played for Ed. During the parents' meeting at the start of each season, Ed always pointed to Dave and said, "He was the captain of my first team here. We had a pretty good year that year, didn't we, Dave?" Dave would smile and say something like, "We sure did, Coach, a great year. And this year is going to be even better." The longer Ed was in Parkersburg, and the more success his teams had, the more pride Dave felt in being the captain of the team that got everything started.

Dave's response was exactly what Ed hoped to accomplish as a coach. From the start, his goals went beyond the game of football. He set out to create a winning tradition, but he didn't measure success in wins and losses. "If all I ever teach you is how to block and tackle, then I have failed you as a coach." Most coaches on all levels say something like this to their teams, but Ed lived it. He cared for his players and students as people, and that did not change after they graduated. Once someone played for him, they were a part of his team for life. On any given day, when he ran into his former players, he immediately greeted them with a hearty, "Boy, it's good to see you. How's your family? Tell me what's going on in your life right now." These weren't rhetorical questions. Ed truly wanted to know what was going on in his players' lives. If things weren't going well, he stopped what he was doing and talked with them about how they could move forward. That may be why people all over town thought of "Coach" as their best friend.

Now as Ed and Todd walked down the streets of Parkersburg on their way to the high school, his "team" was in the worst crisis he'd ever seen. Hundreds of his friends had lost everything they owned. "This is just unbelievable, pal," he said to Todd as they walked along. "Never in my wildest dreams did I think something like this could happen here."

"Yeah, me either," Todd said. "And to think that I went outside to take a look when the sirens went off instead of going into the basement with Candice. I thought the storm would turn out to be nothing. Now look at this."

Ed laughed for the first time since the tornado hit. "I tried to do the same thing, but your mother insisted I go down in the basement instead. I guess it's a good thing she did."

"Uh, yeah, Dad."

❖ ❖ ❖

Aaron made the drive from Dysart to Parkersburg in record time. Once or twice he glanced down at the speedometer in his truck. When he did, he let off the gas pedal just enough to keep his speed under ninety. Even then, police cars flew past him on their way to Parkersburg.

About a mile south of town, Aaron topped a hill on Highway 14 and slammed on his brakes. The road just ahead was closed to everything but emergency traffic. He noticed a gravel road to his left and took off down it. He kept looking north. Off in the distance he saw the Parkersburg water tower, but he could not see anything else. Eventually the gravel road turned north toward town. His truck fishtailed around the ninety-degree curve as he pressed hard on the gas pedal. He sped north up a road that eventually becomes Johnson Street in Parkersburg. Any other day, Johnson Street would have taken him within a half block of his parents' house. This wasn't any other day.

Aaron came up over a rise that gave him his first view of the place he had always taken for granted as home. He slammed on the brakes and threw his truck into park. Tossing the door open, he jumped out and took off toward his parents' house, or at least where he thought his parents' house should be. Even though he was sure he was within a block, maybe two, of their house, nothing looked familiar. "Oh, my gosh," Aaron said, "it's gone. Everything is gone."

Somewhere around the spot where he stood was the yard his dad had turned into the family football stadium on Sunday afternoons for a game they called "touchdown" when Aaron was little. The object of the game was simple enough. Ed played quarterback. Aaron and Todd were the receivers. And Jan was the lone defensive back. Aaron and Todd ran pass patterns around Mom while Dad motioned them to go further. If Aaron and Todd could score a touchdown in four downs, they won. Their mother rarely won the game.

Whenever it was too cold or wet to play football in the yard, Ed put a Nerf ball basketball hoop above one door for a full family game of basketball. Aaron teamed with one parent, Todd with the other, and they went at it. Ed and Jan played on their knees. The games lasted all afternoon, or until Mom and Dad were too exhausted to keep going. The living room also doubled as a football field when Ed came home from work. The moment he walked in the door, Aaron and Todd came running up and tried to tackle him. That game ended once they were big enough not only to tackle him but to hurt him in the process. When the boys were very little, Ed ran practice drills with them right before bedtime. Aaron could still remember doing footfire drills in his footie pajamas when he was maybe four years old.

Now Aaron could not even find the place where the house had once been. Everything he had used as a landmark to find his way around the south side of town as a boy had been rendered unrecognizable.

❖ ❖ ❖

Police cruisers and fire trucks from surrounding towns filled the high school parking lot as Ed and Todd walked up to the school. Ed headed straight to the football field. The school had named it after him a few years earlier. He never called it Ed Thomas Field, just as he never called it the Sacred Acre. From his house he could tell the school had been hit by the tornado, but he wasn't prepared for what he saw as he looked down on the field where his team played ball. Portions of the home grandstands were upended and mangled. The press box lay shattered on the ground. The goalpost in the west end zone looked like a pretzel.

As for the field itself, it looked like a pincushion. Debris from the storm didn't just cover the grass. Two-by-fours and sheets of plywood and glass and lawn mower decks and anything else the EF5 tornado could rip from the houses south of town appeared to have been driven down into the turf with a jackhammer. Tears welled up in Ed's eyes. Todd put his arm around his father, fighting back tears of his own. "It'll be OK, Dad."

Ed took a deep breath. "I know." He stood there for a moment, staring out at the place where he had invested so much of himself. Letting out a long sigh, he said, "I need to get to my classroom."

They turned toward the building. "Dad, we can't go in there. It looks worse than the field," Todd said.*

---

*For glimpses of the damage to the high school and the surrounding area, go to *www.youtube.com/watch?v=z9VPPBa1bY0.*

"I have to at least try," Ed said. Todd didn't try to talk him out of it. If there was one thing he had learned about his father, it was that he never let any obstacle, large or small, get in his way. Once he set his mind to something, he found a way to get it done.

The two of them pushed through a door near what remained of the gym and walked down the main hallway. Portions of the hall itself were clear, but the wall on the left-hand side had collapsed into a classroom. "That room was one of our safe rooms," Ed said, "the place where the kids were supposed to go when the tornado sirens go off."

"Whoa," Todd said. The roof and walls had caved down onto the desks below. "I hate to think what might have happened if the storm had hit when school was in session."

Ed and Todd picked their way through the rubble. They finally made it to the hallway near Ed's classroom. Steel girders that had once supported the roof hung down, blocking their path.

"Hey," a voice called out to them, "it's not safe in there. You need to get out." Ed turned and saw a sheriff's deputy pointing at them.

"Come on, Dad, let's get out of here," Todd said. "You can't do anything in here right now anyway."

Ed sighed and wiped his eyes. "OK, pal. Let's go."

Ed and Todd arrived back at what remained of the Thomases' home. Aaron was wandering around, trying to get his bearings. After hugs and stories of what had just happened, Ed said to his sons, "I really need to go back and try to get into my classroom."

"Dad, we already tried once. That place isn't safe. What's so important that it can't wait?" Todd asked.

"All the booster club money is locked up in my office, along with money for the summer football T-shirts the boys ordered, ticket money, and the cash I set aside for the football program through the year from my speaking engagements," Ed said.

"So are we talking about a thousand dollars?" Todd asked. "That's not worth taking a chance of having a wall fall on you."

Ed lowered his voice. "Closer to forty thousand."

Aaron jumped in. "Why on earth would you have that kind of money in your classroom, Dad?"

Ed just smiled. "That's how I've always done it. I can keep an eye on it that way. Never seemed to present a problem until now."

Aaron and Todd looked at one another and shook their heads. "Yeah, all right, I'll go with you," Aaron said.

The number of emergency vehicles in the school parking lot had increased exponentially since Ed's first foray there an hour or so earlier. He and Aaron walked up to the same entrance he had gone into with Todd. An emergency management official in a bright yellow shirt with an ID badge dangling off the front stepped in front of them. "I'm sorry. This site is restricted. No one is allowed inside," he said.

"Sure, I understand," Ed said, "but I just need to get inside for a minute. I'm Ed Thomas, the football coach ..."

"Yes, sir, I know who you are, but you still aren't going inside the school building. A couple of the walls could collapse at any moment. I cannot allow you to go inside."

"I don't plan on moving in. I have a few things in my room that I absolutely must get out of there," Ed said.

"If anything is left in your room, I can assure you that nobody else will be allowed to get in there and take it. Your things that survived the storm will be fine."

"You don't understand. I have to get in there."

"No, *you* don't understand, Coach Thomas. No one, and I mean no one, can enter this school building. No exceptions. The last thing I'm going to do is let you or anyone else go waltzing in there and have a wall come down on top of you. Case closed."

Ed opened his mouth to say something else, but Aaron cut him off. "Come on, Dad. You're not going to win this argument."

Reluctantly, Ed gave in. He allowed Aaron to pull him by the arm away from the gym entrance. The two of them walked just out of earshot of the emergency management official. "OK, follow me,"

Ed said. "I think we can get in back by the shop." They rounded a corner, and Ed stopped. "Well, will you look at that." He was right about being able to get in through the shop. The shop, along with the entire back side of the school building, was completely gone.

Once inside, they crawled around, under and over rubble, until they reached Ed's classroom. Desks were upended. Steel girders hung down, twisted. Ceiling tiles and roofing material covered the floor.

Ed walked over to a pile that sat where his desk was supposed to be. "Can you give me a hand?" he said. Aaron helped his father lift a board of broken Sheetrock off the side of the desk so they could get to the drawers. He had never seen his father so shaken, so in shock.

Ed dug around through a couple of the drawers. "This is unbelievable, you know it? Just unbelievable." He let out a long sigh. "OK, here they are," he said, pulling out the money boxes.

"OK, Dad, can we get out of here?" Aaron said.

"Yeah. I'm done," Ed said. On the way out he also grabbed his playbooks, along with some of the framed photographs of former players that still hung on the walls.

"Dad," Aaron said.

"OK, really, I'm done now."

CHAPTER 3

A STORM OF DOUBT

Adversity is the test of character.
ED THOMAS

JAN LOST ALL SENSE OF TIME IN THE IMMEDIATE AFTERMATH of the tornado. From the moment she found her shoes under a pile of rubble and took off running in the general direction of the fire station, she had been locked on task. Other EMTs and firefighters arrived at the station shortly after she did. Jan took charge. While Ed was digging through the rubble of his classroom, she helped move debris from the ambulance station so that they could put the ambulances into service. She then turned the station garage into a staging area for the injured. Since all of the roads on the south side of town were impassable, those who were injured had to make their way to the station for help. Most walked. Many were transported on the back of four-wheelers. One young mother came rushing up, carrying her two-year-old daughter. "You've got to help my little girl," she demanded. Jan thought the mother might hyperventilate at any moment.

"Where is she hurt?" Jan asked.

"How should I know?" the woman shrieked. "That's why I brought her here. Our house just blew away from around us!"

"Yes, ma'am," Jan said. She took the girl by the hand. "OK, let me take a look." The mother bounced from foot to foot, crying, moaning. Jan focused on the two-year-old. Dirt streaked the girl's skin, along with a few minor cuts and bruises. Jan ran her hands up each arm. "Does this hurt, sweetie?" she asked. The girl shook her head no. Pulling a penlight out of her EMT bag, Jan checked the girl's pupils for signs of a concussion. She asked a few basic questions, and the girl answered every one. After a few minutes of tests, Jan patted the girl on the head and said to her mother, "Her injuries appear to be minor."

"NO!" the mother yelled. "You put her in an ambulance and take her to the hospital where she can be checked out by a DOCTOR! DO YOU HEAR ME!"

"I'm sorry, but with so many injured people and only two ambulances, we can only transport those with the most critical injuries."

That was not the response the mother wanted. She launched into a profanity-laced tirade, calling Jan every name in the book. Jan calmly took it. "I understand your wanting to have your daughter checked by a doctor. I believe you probably should, but we cannot take an ambulance out of service for an extended period of time for a non-life-threatening injury. There are people around here with cars that are still drivable who will happily take you to the hospital in Cedar Falls if you ask," Jan said, still calm, no matter how angry the panicked mom became.

"WHAT IF THIS WAS YOUR CHILD?"

"I would say the same thing."

Finally, the child's grandmother pulled the mother away. They did not return.

Aaron saw his mother for the first time the night of the tornado around 9:30. He thought he was looking at his father on game night. She had the same tunnel-vision focus that his dad had while trying to shut down an opponent's offense. A second tornado could have dropped down next to her and it wouldn't have rattled her. He walked over to his friend Chris Luhring. Chris was the chief of police. "Whoa, I've never seen my mom like that," Aaron said.

"Yep, she has been amazing."

"So who's in charge here?" Aaron asked.

Chris laughed. "Officially? Me. In reality? You're looking at her."

"Can we do anything?"

"You and your dad might stay close by in case I have to go look at somebody"—that is, if he had to go identify a body found by a rescuer combing through the wreckage, house by house. Chris had practically grown up in the Thomases' home. He and Aaron attended school together from preschool on up. In high school, Aaron played quarterback, and Chris was a split end—although in Ed Thomas's offense, that meant Aaron handed the ball off to a running back and Chris blocked. Even so, the two had been friends forever. If Chris had to go identify any bodies in the night, he wanted someone he could trust nearby. He especially wanted Coach close by. Chris loved Ed like a father.

After a while it became clear that almost everyone was accounted for. The state police evacuated the town. Everyone except for emergency personnel was supposed to be out of Parkersburg by 9:00 p.m. Aaron and Ed were two of the last to leave. After checking on Jan at the ambulance station, they headed toward Aaron's in-laws' house, five miles north of town.

Sometime around 10:30, Ed collapsed into a chair at the dining room table in the home of Ellie's parents, Jerry and Janet Junker. He let out a long sigh. "You know," he said looking up at Ellie, "I think this is the first time I've sat down since before five o'clock this afternoon, except for riding in Aaron's truck on the way over here."

"You have to be exhausted," Ellie said.

"I am. I didn't realize how tired I was until I sat down. Whew, what a day," he said. Ellie walked over and gave him a hug. As she did, tears welled up in Ed's eyes. "You know, it's weird," he said. "At the end of the day, I usually end up dozing off in my recliner in front of a ball game in my living room. And now all that is gone." Ed dropped his head, his shoulders slumped down. "I can't believe I don't have a place to call home." He began to weep. "I can't believe I don't have a place to call home."

Ellie opened her mouth as if to say something, but the words stuck in the back of her throat. Instead of talking, she hugged her father-in-law tighter. One thing she admired about Ed, something she had admired about him since she was a student at A-P, was his willingness to show his emotions. A dozen years earlier in the championship game, when she and Aaron were seniors, A-P came within a bad second half of finishing the year as undefeated state champions. At a pep rally filled with students and parents after the game, tears streamed down Ed's cheeks as he told the crowd how he thanked God for the privilege of coaching that group of young people. The entire crowd choked up when he said, "There's always going to be a winner, and there's always going to be a loser, but only on the scoreboard. You can tell the true champions by how they handle themselves in adversity. And these young people today handled themselves like champions after we lost to a very good football team." That pep rally never seemed further away.

Not much else was said that night. Ed took a shower and went off to bed not long after arriving at the Junkers' home. Jan spent the night at the ambulance station. It would be another day before she would get any real sleep.

Sometime around eight o'clock the following morning, Chris Luhring drove his four-wheel-drive Ford Explorer squad car to the Thomases' house. Like Jan, Chris had worked through the night, and so had his Explorer. Given the way he had abused it over the past fifteen hours, he was more than a little surprised it was still running and that all four tires weren't flat. When the tornado hit, he was at his in-laws' farm a few miles north of Parkersburg. For the first time in a long time, he had taken the day off completely. He didn't have his police radio or pager or even his cell phone with him. Instead, he wanted to clear his mind as he worked in the garden, thinking about anything but his job. Even when the rain started to fall, he stayed outside, listening to the rolls of thunder off in the distance. He had needed a day like that for a very long time.

News reports on the radio of the approaching tornado ended his day off. He arrived in Parkersburg just after the storm had passed. Approaching from the north, he saw the water tower in the distance, which was a good sign. The north side of town looked fairly normal as well. A few trees had damage, but all in all, the town appeared to have come through unscathed. Then he turned a corner and saw his uncle's house lying in the middle of the street. Immediately, he took off toward his sister and brother-in-law's house. From what he could see, it appeared their house lay right in the path of the worst of the tornado. Dropping his Explorer into four-wheel drive, he drove over trees, toppled roofs, telephone poles, anything that lay in his path. He came up to a relative's house, or what had been their house, and saw that they were OK. However, they started yelling at Chris and waving their arms. Finally he stopped the Explorer and hollered, "What?"

"You're dragging a tree behind you," someone said.

"So?" Chris said, "I've got people I have to get to! I'll deal with the tree later." He then took off, climbing over utility poles and shattered walls, a tree in tow.

Those first few moments immediately after the storm defined the rest of his day and night. Fifteen hours later, he was still at it, although rather than running in search-and-rescue gear, he was now trying to manage the flow of rescuers and family members of storm victims inside and outside of town, along with overseeing salvage operations and stopping looters. With the latter, out-of-towners, not locals, were the problem. Any time a disaster hits, a few people look at it as a chance to go on a free shopping spree. Even though the state police had every road in and out of town blocked, rumor had it that a set of looters came into town on a raft up the river. Chris always tried to see the best in people, but in this case he had trouble believing anyone could be so callous.

He pulled up to the Thomases' house on official business. Ed,

Aaron, Ellie, Todd, and a few other people were busy digging through debris. Jan was still at the fire station, although she would join the family a little later that morning. Chris pulled up and rolled down his window. "Hey, Coach," he said.

Ed walked over to Chris's Explorer. The sight of Chris allowed Ed to drop his guard. Tears began rolling down his face. That broke the dam Chris had held back for the past fifteen hours. He began to weep as well. Ed stuck his head inside the passenger side window of the vehicle. The first words out of his mouth were, "I don't know if I can do this."

The sound of those words surprised Chris as much as the news that an EF5 tornado had plowed through Parkersburg. "What, Coach? I mean, you have to ..."

"I know, Chris, but I don't know if I can."

"All my life, Coach, you've told me that adversity is the true test of character. You've shown me how to never let the storms define who I am. You've always done that, always, Coach." Chris's voice began to crack. He could barely force words out of his mouth. "This can't be a question of whether or not you can; it is a question of when you will start. You have to show us the way, Coach, just like you always have."

"But ...," Ed could barely speak, "we've never been through anything like this before. I just heard that six people died. My neighbor Chuck didn't make it. He has lived behind me for years, and now he's gone." Ed looked down at the ground, tears flowing faster than before. "I never thought something like this was possible here. Never."

Chris shook his head. "I know, Coach; I know." He paused, searching for the right words. "I could spend a million dollars a day here to rebuild everything, but it won't mean a thing unless you lead us."

Ed didn't say anything. He looked over at the rubble of his house. Aaron and Ellie were down on their knees, picking through a pile of boards, Sheetrock, and insulation. Ellie's parents each had a rake, combing through materials near what appeared to be the garage. After a few moments, Ed said, "Can you give me a lift over to the high school?"

"Sure."

Ed climbed in, and Chris put the Explorer into gear. "Uh, you know, speaking of the high school, that's why I came over to see you."

"How's that?"

"A state police officer called me from over at the school. He told me that if you come into the school building one more time, he's going to arrest you."

"What?" Ed seemed genuinely taken aback. "So what did you tell him?"

"I told them to do what they have to do, but that I would deal with you."

"So are you here to deal with me?" Ed said.

"I guess. So listen. I'm the incident co-commander of this mess, which means I'm pretty much in charge. If you need to get back in your classroom, don't just go waltzing over there and try to sneak in through a hole in the wall or something. You find me, and I'll take you inside. OK?"

"Well," Ed said, "now that you mention it ..."

"Sure, Coach. Whatever you need. I have time."

Forty-five minutes and a carload of items from Ed's classroom later, Chris drove him back home. "Thanks, Chris, for everything," Ed said as he grabbed the car door handle.

"Coach, I meant what I said. We can rebuild this town. We can spend ten million dollars here and put everything back as good as new, but that won't be enough for this town to recover. After every loss, what did you say to us? You said adversity shapes character."

"That's not fair, using my own words against me," Ed said.

"They were never just words. My whole life I've watched you live them. I know you will now too. I mean, who knows? This storm may be why God brought you here in the first place. You told me the school was your church, your mission field. Well, there are a lot of people in this town who went through your church and are looking to you to see what you're going to do now."

Ed sat silently for a moment, taking it all in. Finally, he turned to Chris, slapped him on the thigh, and said, "Thanks. And thanks for not arresting me." With that, he laughed, climbed out of the car, and went back to picking through the rubble of his house with his family.

That afternoon, Chris dropped by the incident command center at the fire station for a cup of coffee and a sandwich. He took a few bites of his sandwich and flopped down on the ground to rest. On the nearby radio he heard a familiar voice. He listened more closely and heard Coach Thomas tell a reporter from a Cedar Falls station, "The principal and the superintendent and I got together earlier, and the three of us decided that, God willing, we will play our first home game right here on our field right on schedule."

A smile broke out across Chris's face. *We're going to come through this*, he thought to himself. *We're going to be all right.* He reached for his cup and took a sip of his coffee. Then another thought hit him. *Holy crap, how long until the first home game? Three months? How on earth are we going to pull* that *off?*

If there was one thing Chris Luhring loved about Ed Thomas, it was that Coach never dreamed small. When he set a goal, it was always profound. Chris had never met anyone who could get a group of people to dream so big and so wide and so crazy. But he had also never met anyone so gifted at showing you how to reach your goals and then leading you to do it.

"Coach is back. We're going to be all right," he said with a smile. "Yep, Coach is back!"

CHAPTER 4

"WE WILL REBUILD"

*The greatest gift God has given any
of us is the power to choose.*
ED THOMAS

ED'S FATHER WAS AN ALCOHOLIC; HIS MOTHER WAS A DEVOUT
Christian. Arthurine Whyle didn't realize she had married an alcoholic when she said "I do." During their courtship, Roy Thomas
went to church every single Sunday with her. One Sunday, he went
forward during the altar call and said he gave his life to Jesus Christ.

Everything changed after their wedding day. Once they were
married, Roy spent less and less time at church and more and more
time with his old buddies down at the local tavern. He never drank
at home because Arthurine did not allow liquor inside the walls of
her house. That didn't stop Roy from drinking, and his drinking
did not stop Arthurine from pursuing her relationship with Christ.
Every time the church doors were open, she was there. What Cheer,
Iowa, was a small town where everyone knows everyone else's business, but that never seemed to bother Arthurine. She did not hide
in embarrassment over her husband's drinking, nor did she ever
make excuses for him. In her eyes, life was what it was. She married a man who turned out to be something other than what she
had believed. Rather than moan over her lot in life or break off her
marriage, she chose to go forward. At home she loved her husband.

In church she prayed for the day God would turn Roy's heart back to himself.

By the time Ed, their first child, came along, Roy ended up at the tavern almost every evening after work. Most nights he came home drunk. Roy worked hard and tried to provide for his family, but his drinking made things tighter than they should have been. On the weekends, Roy brought Ed into town with him to pick up seed at the local mill and to buy supplies for the farm on which they lived. Ed adored his dad. Even so, most trips ultimately ended up at the tavern. However, before Roy headed off to the bar with his buddies, he dropped Ed off at Arthurine's parents' house.

Ed loved his grandparents. As a little boy, he rode along with his grandfather as he delivered bread from the family bakery to all the houses in What Cheer. After his grandfather died, Ed spent nearly as much time with his grandmother as he did at his own home. From the time he was a young boy, she had him memorize Bible verses. Before she let him run outside to play, she pulled him over to her side and said, "Edward, did you learn your verse today?" He shook his head yes, which always led to her saying, "OK, let's hear it." With that, Ed quickly recited John 3:16 or Romans 3:23 — or whatever verse she had assigned him that day. "Very good. That's perfect," she said as he rattled off every line exactly as it was written in the King James Version. That put a smile on his face, and he ran out the door to play ball.

When he was in the sixth grade, his grandmother asked him, "Edward, how would you like to read through the Bible together, you and me?"

"The whole thing?"

"Yes, the whole thing. A little every day until we get to the end."

"OK," he replied. "That sounds like a good idea."

The family had moved into town by then, and so Ed started walking over to his grandmother's house every day for Bible reading. The two of them sat down on the couch, opened the Bible, and alternated reading it out loud, verse by verse, one or two chapters at a time. They did this every day until they worked their way from Genesis to Revelation. There were days when Ed forgot and headed off to the ball field. Before long, a little green Plymouth pulled up next to the sandlot and honked its horn. "Hey, guys, it's my grandmother. I gotta go," he called out to his buddies. "I'll be back in a little while." Then it was off to Grandma's house.

Some twelve-year-old boys might have thought of this as a cruel form of punishment. Not Ed. All his life he talked about how much he learned from reading through the Bible with his grandmother. He thought everyone who is serious about being a Christian should read through the Bible. And he was more serious about being a Christian than he was about anything else in his life.

Ed got that from his mother. For her, life wasn't very complicated. Arthurine Teresa Whyle Thomas had a black-and-white way of looking at the world, a trait her oldest child inherited. When you know the right thing to do, you do it. If you know something is wrong, you don't do it. When she found candy in one of her daughter's pockets—candy Arthurine knew she hadn't given to her—she confronted her. "Where did you get this candy, Connie?" she asked her three-year-old daughter.

"The store."

"Did someone buy the candy for you?"

Connie shook her head no.

"Did you take the candy?"

Connie nodded her head yes. Next thing they knew, Arthurine had all the kids in the car and headed back to the local drugstore to make things right. She didn't think anything of what she did, although her daughter never forgot it. Returning stolen pieces of penny candy is what you do if you claim to be a Christian. Arthurine taught her children that every day you face a choice. Either you choose to do what is right, or you choose to do what is wrong. When you choose to do the right thing, you set yourself up for good things to happen. But when you choose to do the wrong thing, consequences follow. And if you suffer the consequences of your own poor choices, you cannot moan and complain. Instead you must learn from your mistakes and move forward.

Arthurine was the spiritual leader of her home, and she led by example. She took the children to church, read the Bible to them, and corrected them when they got in trouble. As the oldest child, Ed assumed more and more of that role as he matured. In high school, he became a junior deacon and helped with Communion at their local church. Sunday afternoons, he dragged his two sisters with him to the young people's service, although only one or two other kids went. That didn't matter to Ed. He was like his mother in that he figured if the pastor went to the trouble of having a special event for teenagers on a Sunday afternoon, he needed to be there, and so did his sisters.

Even as he assumed more and more of the role of setting an example for his two sisters, and later for a sister and his only brother who were born right around the time he finished high school, Ed still leaned on his mother. Each night when he went to bed, he called down to her from his room in a voice so loud that everyone could hear him. "Hey, Mom," he said, "would you say a short prayer?"

"Of course, Edward," she said. She then proceeded to pray out loud for each and every member of the family by name. When she finished, Ed called out, "Thanks, Mom," and then he went to sleep. He did this up until the day he left for college.

Ed grew up between two worlds. On the one hand, he had the world of his mother. Sundays and Wednesdays they went to church. The rest of the week she hauled all her children around to Ed's ball games, even though she didn't have a clue as to what was taking place on the field.

On the other hand, there was his father. Ed could count on one hand the number of times his dad showed up at church or at one of Ed's games. On the nights Roy came home drunk, the entire family cringed, especially Ed. He avoided having friends over on the nights his father went out drinking. His dad usually came in, cursing and carrying on, two things Ed found unconscionable. Ed's mother did her best to coax Roy upstairs and out of sight as quickly as possible, but for Ed and his sisters, the damage was done.

While it would have been easy for him to resent his father, Ed didn't. He felt embarrassed *for* him, not *by* him. All his life, Ed chose to see the best in people. He refused to believe anyone was a victim of their past or their circumstances. That is why Ed saw more in his father than his father saw in himself. Ed knew that Roy was capable of so much more, if only he would choose to walk away from the alcohol that controlled his life.

When Ed was eighteen, that choice was made for his father. One Sunday afternoon, Roy went over to a cousin's house, and the two of them did their best to get as drunk as possible as quickly as possible. That in and of itself was nothing unusual. They drank together on a regular basis. However, that afternoon did not turn out like all the rest. After a few rounds, the two of them starting talking about the old days, back when they were kids. "You know, I could always take you," Roy said.

His cousin took the bait. "Roy, you must be drunk, because you know you couldn't take me on *my* worst day and *your* best." The two of them went back and forth verbally for a while, all in fun, until one of them made the first move. They began wrestling around the yard. Ed's father got the worst of it. He fell awkwardly on his head and screamed out in pain. His arms and legs would not move.

The phone rang at the Thomases' house. Ed's mother answered, listened closely to the voice on the other end, and then informed the family, "We have to get to the hospital. Your father has been in an accident." After they arrived at the hospital, the family was told Roy might not survive. "His neck is broken, Mrs. Thomas," the doctor said. "He is paralyzed from the neck down. It may or may not be permanent. We just don't know yet."

Roy Thomas eventually regained full use of his arms and legs, yet the experience left him changed. During his four months in the hospital, he went through deep withdrawal from alcohol. Once he went home, he never drank again. Although Roy didn't become a churchgoing man, he became engaged in his two youngest children's lives in a way he never had been for Ed or for Roy's two oldest daughters. Roy rarely made it to one of Ed's games, but he never missed one of Ed's little brother Greg's games. Ed never resented the father Greg and Teresa enjoyed. If anything, he felt a great deal of pride over the man Roy had become. Ed always knew he had it in him. The changes in Roy's life made a huge difference in Ed's relationship with his dad. Roy may not have attended the games Ed played, but he made sure he watched his oldest son coach his first game, and as many games as he could after that.

Living between these two worlds, and watching what happened when they collided, left Ed with two lifelong convictions that shaped everything he did. First, his mother showed him how the greatest power God gives any of us is the power to choose. Ed watched his mother choose to love his father, even as he was doing so much to make himself hard to love. She chose to stick with him and love him, and good things happened as a result. Granted, it took a broken neck for her husband to change, but that experience is what left Ed with his second conviction: Adversity not only reveals character; it shapes it if we let it. Ed's father showed that when something bad happens, you choose how you will respond to it. When you make the right choice, adversity becomes a tremendous opportunity rather than a problem to be solved. His father seized that opportunity, gave up drinking, and became a new man. Ed admired his father for what he did, and he never forgot the lesson he learned through the experience.

❖ ❖ ❖

Forty years later, Ed stood with Ron Westerman at the top of the stairs on the hill that led down to the football field. It was the day after the tornado ripped through Parkersburg. Ron worked as the head custodian at the middle school. A couple of years earlier, Ed roped Ron into helping lay sod on part of the high school football field, and Ron was hooked. Soon Ed dragged Ron along with him to turf conventions all over the state. In the past year, Ron started turning the middle school field into his own version of the Sacred Acre.

The two of them stood looking over the high school field, silently, for a few moments, staring at the twisted goalposts and the two-by-fours sticking up from the turf like porcupine spines. Finally Ron said, "Coach, what an opportunity we have."

Ed smiled. "We sure do." He pointed out toward the far side of the field. "You know, we've complained for a long time about pulling weeds along that fence line. I don't see a fence now. Problem solved," he said.

"So what's next?"

"Rebuild and play our first home game right here, right on schedule."

"This season?"

"Has to be this season," Ed said. "*Has* to be. Getting it done in time won't be easy. But you know, there's a huge gap between really hard and impossible. I figure this job lies right in there, so we'll get it done."

As the two talked, school superintendent Jon Thompson and high school principal Dave Meyers walked over to them. The two had just completed a walking tour of the school. "Hey, Ed," Jon said.

"Hey, Jon. So how does it look to you?" Ed asked.

"I'd say it's a total loss. The insurance guy said something about maybe being able to salvage the south wing, but I don't see how. To me, the only thing we can do is tear down what's left standing, clear the deck, and rebuild from the ground up."

"I think that's a good choice. It would be harder to make what's left usable than it would be to start over from scratch," Ed said. "You know, the school was maybe five years old when I came here in 1975. Makes me sick to think about tearing it down, but it's the right choice."

Dave added, "Everyone is so afraid that the kids are all going to get shipped out to Dike or Grundy Center or one of the other nearby districts. We want to get the word out that none of us are going anywhere. The school is going to be rebuilt right where it was, and we're going to do our level best to get it done in time for the start of school one year from now."

Ed smiled. "That sounds great to me. And while you're getting the word out, you might as well tell everybody that we're going to play our first home football game on our own field as scheduled this season."

Jon did a double take. "What? Wait a minute. You mean *next* season, don't you, Ed, when the new school is up?"

"No. I mean *this* season. Our first home game is 104 days from today. We open the week before on the road against Dike-New Hartford, and then we will be here for our home opener against West Marshall the next week. We will play that game right here on our own field, right on schedule."

Jon looked down at the football field. "Come on, Ed, be serious."

Ed looked the superintendent in the eye. "I am serious. Think about what that's going to do for the entire community. We need this. The people of this town—they need some normalcy while they try to put their lives back together." Ed began to tear up as he spoke. "Parkersburg needs something that lets them know that this storm did not beat us and will not define who we are."

Dave smiled. Jon shook his head, but he didn't argue the point with Ed. He knew better than to try to talk him out of it, and he also knew better than to doubt the fact that the Aplington-Parkersburg Falcons would indeed play their first home game in a newly rebuilt Ed Thomas Field, right on schedule. A year earlier, the superintendent and his wife attended the mandatory preseason football parents' meeting. Their son played quarterback for Ed. In the meeting, Ed laid out his plans for the season to all the moms and dads. After thirty minutes of listening to Ed speak, Jon's wife turned to him and said, "I wanna go tackle somebody!" The way Jon saw it, if Ed Thomas could move a middle-aged woman to want to put on a set of shoulder pads and a helmet in less than thirty minutes, he could certainly get a new football field built and ready to go in 104 days.

"OK, Ed," Jon said. He let out a quick sigh. "That's what we will do. We're going to build the school from the ground up in one year's time, and we're going to play our first home football game here in 104 days. Wow, I think that settles it. We have officially lost our minds."

"No, Jon, we've just set ourselves a good set of goals. If you're going to set a goal, you might as well set one worth fighting for," Ed said.

Ed didn't come out and say it, but his bold pronouncement on the hill grew out of his trust in the power and goodness of God, a trust formed while growing up between two very different worlds. Lots of tears were yet to be shed over all that the storm had taken away, and the shock of losing everything had not yet fully subsided. But Ed never wavered in his conviction that God presented him and the entire community with a choice as to how they would respond. For Ed, like everything connected with his work at the school, this was not about football. This was about choosing to trust in God's wisdom and plan, even though he did not fully understand how or why God would allow such a devastating storm. Many of those who lost everything wondered how a good God could allow such a tragedy to hit their little town. Ed never did, just as he never heard his mother question why God would allow her to be duped into marrying a man who was not what he made himself out to be. Instead, she trusted God and put her husband in his hands. That's what Ed chose to do after the initial shock of the tornado devastation wore off.

One week after the tornado, Ed and Jan attended worship at First Congregational Church of Parkersburg, just as they did every

61

Sunday. During the worship service, their pastor asked if anyone would like to share a testimony. Ed stepped up to the microphone. "First Timothy 6:7 tells us that we come into this world with nothing, and we leave the same way," he began. "Thank God, I did not leave this world last Sunday, but Jan and I, like a lot of you, lost everything we had. I'm here to tell you that losing everything is not such a horrible thing. I'm not saying this has been any easier for me than it has for any of you, and I will grieve for a very long time over my neighbors and friends who lost their lives Sunday. But I have to tell you, over these past six days, I've seen the mercy and goodness of God through people he has sent our way like nothing I've ever seen.

"I've also rediscovered over this past week how our faith in God is the only thing that is going to carry us through these times. You know, Job also lost everything he had in a tornado, only he also lost his children, something that I hope I never have to experience. After he lost everything, he told his wife, 'Naked I came into this world, and naked I will depart. The Lord gives. The Lord takes away. Blessed be the name of the Lord.'* Job praised God in the storm, and that's what I want to be able to do as well.

"God was with Jan and me down in our basement while our house blew away. I've heard stories from a lot of you of how you felt like the wind was about to suck you right out of your shelter when something reached out and pulled you back down to safety. Well, that something was the hand of God. He was with us through the storm, and he will be with us as we get up and go forward and rebuild this community. Thank you."

Ed walked off the platform and took his seat next to Jan. Thirty-three years earlier, God brought Ed to Parkersburg and gave him a job to do. Nothing had changed that fact—not even an EF5 tornado. In fact, his work had just begun.

---

*Job 1:21.

CHAPTER 5

STARTING OVER

*The only way we win
is to look out for one another.*
ED THOMAS

EARLY IN THEIR FIRST YEAR OF MARRIAGE, ED STAYED UP late to watch a ball game one night while Jan went to bed without him. Ed didn't know that Jan had spent most of the afternoon rearranging the furniture in their small duplex, nor did he notice that the bed and dresser had swapped places when he came home that afternoon and changed his clothes. Once the game finally ended, Ed clicked off the television and headed off to the bedroom. As he walked down the hall, a devious little idea hatched in his mind. Quietly, he opened the bedroom door. He crept over across the room in the darkness, and then he suddenly dove toward the bed, or at least where he thought the bed was supposed to be.

Jan sat straight up in bed when she heard a loud thump, which was followed by a moan. She switched on a lamp only to find Ed curled up and rolling on the ground, the wind knocked out of him. "What are you doing?"

When Ed finally got his breath back, he said, "I was going to play a little trick on you, but it didn't exactly turn out the way I planned. What happened to the bed?"

Jan could not help but laugh. "I moved it when I cleaned the bedroom today. Remember, you sat on it this afternoon when you came home from work."

"I did? I don't remember that. Why do you have to move things all the time, anyway?"

"I like variety."

"I don't," Ed said, still on the floor.

"Then you better pay closer attention around here," Jan countered with a playful tone.

Ed stumbled to his feet, his pride damaged but his sense of humor intact. "At least warn me next time," he said with a chuckle.

In the week that followed the tornado, Ed never found his bed or most of his other possessions. He and Jan, along with Aaron, Todd, and several other family volunteers, spent hours upon hours digging through the scattered debris that now represented everything they had in the world. Any hopes that they might actually find things intact fell apart when they uncovered one of the dressers from their bedroom. Even though the drawers were closed tight, dirt and insulation were deeply embedded in socks and sweaters and every other piece of clothing. Jan soon discovered that even a thousand trips through the washer and dryer would never get it all out.

Even so, in those first few days, the Thomases loaded as many of their possessions as they could find into the horse trailer Jan's dad brought over for them to use. When Jan uncovered her washer and dryer, she yelled out like she had just won the lottery. "Ha, look what I found!" Aaron and Todd came over and carried the washer and dryer to the trailer. Neither had the heart to tell their mother that both machines were too far gone to ever work again.

For Ed and Jan, like every other storm victim, finding something as simple as a washing machine felt like getting a small part of their lives back. Their biggest celebration came when they uncovered some old photographs of Aaron and Todd, and especially when they found photographs of the grandchildren. Somewhere in the debris, Jan managed to dig out their insurance papers. That first day they also saved a dining room table with large bubbles sticking up in its veneer top, a desk that was missing two drawers, and a wooden dresser that looked like it had been left outside in a thunderstorm. Aside from a few pairs of jeans and a handful of shirts, most of their clothes were either gone forever or ruined. Everything else they needed—from such simple things as socks, toothbrushes, makeup, and razors to big-ticket items like their cars, appliances, and furniture—they had to buy new. Every material item they always took for granted was now scattered between Parkersburg and New Hartford, nine miles away. After thirty-two years of marriage, Ed and Jan had to start over from scratch.

✦ ✦ ✦

Two days after the tornado hit, Ed walked up after a brief trip to the high school. Jan was just finishing a conversation on her cell phone. "You're not going to believe this," she said to Ed, "but I just got off the phone with a contractor."

She caught Ed off guard. He almost said, "Why do we need a contractor?" but he caught himself. Twenty-four hours earlier, hiring a builder was the last thing he could imagine doing.

"I gave Mom the name, Dad," Todd said. "He's actually one of my buddies from college. He does great work, and you can trust him to do what he says. He's going to build my house out by the golf course later this year."

"OK," Ed said, still trying to come to grips with the fact that he needed to rebuild a house.

"He told me that they just finished a house over in Cedar Falls, and they have a window of time before they start on their next one. He and his crew can get started on our house right away," Jan said.

"What do you mean *right away*?" Ed asked.

"As in tomorrow, if we want him to. I told him I had to talk to our insurance company first."

"But any thinking person can see the house is a total loss, so that shouldn't be a problem," Todd added.

"No, it shouldn't be a problem," Jan said, "but …"

Ed jumped in. "So let's hire Todd's buddy and get him out here, the quicker the better."

"I don't know, Ed. I'm not so sure it's a good idea to hire someone so fast without getting bids from several different places first. I mean, come on, we're talking about rebuilding our entire house. I think we need to do our homework before we jump into anything."

"Todd's already checked him out, right? For me, the quicker we rebuild the better. I think it's important for us to send a message to the rest of the community. When I was over at the school …"

"Which time?" Jan interrupted.

Ed smiled. "I just needed to get a few things out of my classroom. Anyways, when I was over at the school, some parents came over with their kids, and a lot of them wondered what was going to happen to the town and if the school would even be rebuilt or if the state might consolidate us with another district. I think it's important to make a statement that we *will* rebuild our town and our school and that we will be better and stronger than before."

"That's fine, Ed, but I'm not so sure it's a good idea to give someone the go-ahead to build a house without so much as a formal bid."

"Todd trusts him. That's good enough for me," Ed said.

"We'll see," Jan said.

That the school and community came into the discussion was not a surprise to Jan. The two had played a major role in Ed and Jan's relationship since the day he first asked her out on a date a few months after she graduated from Northeast Hamilton High School. Back then, Ed was Mr. Thomas, the boys' football coach and her former world history teacher and assistant basketball coach. He came to Northeast Hamilton when she was a junior. Back then, neither ever thought of the other as anything other than a teacher and student. That never would have changed if not for a mutual friend who planted a bug in Ed's ear about Jan after she graduated from high school. He kept telling Ed to give her a call, and he continually built up Ed to Jan. Even so, she felt more than a little strange when she answered her phone and heard her former teacher say, "Hi, this is Ed Thomas."

"OK, hi," Jan said. She did not know what to call him. "Ed" felt far too informal, and "Mr. Thomas" was out of the question. She decided to call him nothing at all.

"I was wondering if you would be interested in going out with me Friday night after the football game?"

If their mutual friend had not warned her in advance that Ed was going to ask her out, Jan would have turned him down flat. After all, who goes out on a date with one of her teachers, even a former teacher after you graduated? Instead she decided to give it a whirl and said, "Sure, that sounds like fun."

"Great," Ed said. "If you don't mind, would you meet me at the school? I have to get there pretty early with the team and all. I'll meet you as soon as the game is over."

"That will be fine. I'll see you then."

"OK, great. Bye, Jan."

"Bye, uh ... er ... bye."

After the initial shock of the phone call wore off, Jan started to warm up to the idea of going out with Ed. After all, he was only a few years older, and, now that she started thinking of him as a man rather than a teacher, she found him attractive. Even so, going out with the girls' basketball assistant coach felt a little odd, so much so that she didn't give much thought to the fact that their first date was wrapped around a Friday night football game, a game her date spent on the sidelines coaching the losing team.

After the final gun sounded and the game ended, Jan went down to an area near the school office where high school kids wait to be picked up by their parents. There she waited. And waited. And waited. "Wow, this is not funny," she said to herself, sure she had been stood up. About the time she decided to go home and chalk it up to bad luck, Ed walked over. "I'm sorry I'm late," he said. "My family came over from What Cheer to watch the game and then they came into the locker room. I couldn't get away. Thanks for waiting for me."

"That's fine," she said. Try as hard as she might, she still could not bring herself to call him Ed.

"There's a faculty party going on right now that I really have to go to. Do you mind if we go there instead of going out to eat?"

"No, not at all," Jan said. This date had just shot over the top on the awkward meter. Here she was, a college freshman who had graduated from this very high school less than six months earlier, attending a faculty party as the date of one of the teachers. After the faculty party, she surprised herself by saying yes when Ed asked if she would like to go out to eat and to see a movie the next night. The second date turned into a third, and the third into a fourth, and before long, the two of them were officially an item. It helped that she learned to call him Ed instead of calling him nothing at all.

Jan wasn't the only member of her family who found this dating arrangement amazingly awkward. Her younger sister, Kim, was still a student at Northeast Hamilton when her big sister started dating her geography teacher. At school, Kim called him Mr. Thomas, and then she came home in the evenings to find him sitting on the couch in her living room, watching television, holding her sister's hand. Kim tried not to think about what was happening and rushed upstairs as quickly as she could. The following summer she had "Mr. Thomas" for driver's ed. Her life had just gone from bad to worse. Kim had no idea what to call him most of the time. Ed never felt awkward. When he saw Kim at Jan's house, he teased her, saying things like, "You're going to fail driver's ed. You're the worst driver in our car." Then he would laugh and let her know it was all a joke. Kim knew he was joking because *she* wasn't the worst driver in the car; *he* was. Ed's poor driving was legendary in northeastern Iowa.

Early on, many of Jan and Ed's dates consisted of her helping him make big motivational posters that he hung in his team's locker room. He picked up a pizza, and they spread the paper and paint across his living room and went to work. In the spring, they went to his softball games and then went out to eat with other couples. Ed may not have been a romantic as far as planning their nights out, but Jan found him to be very thoughtful and kind. He made her laugh, and she enjoyed their time together. On Sundays, they went to church together and then spent the afternoon hanging out with her family. Some Sundays, they drove over to What Cheer to spend time with his family. His mother was anxious to meet this girl about whom Ed's first words were, "Mom, she can palm a basketball!"

When they had been dating less than a year, Ed told Jan he had taken a job at a new school an hour away. "I'll be back every weekend," he promised, "and I will call every night." After he received his first phone bill, he had to scale back to calling two or three nights a week. The long-distance bill took a toll on his teacher's paycheck. However, neither one of them could endure the long-distance relationship for long. That Christmas he proposed, and she accepted. They were married prior to the start of the following football season.

Ed might not have been able to get the Parkersburg job without Jan's help. She didn't come along on any of the interviews, and he didn't seek her opinion on the place, since they were just dating and not engaged. However, something odd happened the fall they started dating. His teams began to win, and win big. Jan never suggested plays to Ed, but a few days before every game, he asked her, "How do you feel about this one?" She gave him her honest answer, and he took her advice to heart. He kept right on asking before every game for the next thirty-four years. Eventually he even had Jan watch game film with him on Saturdays after a Friday night game. She told him what she thought of certain plays and players, and he listened. Something about that combination worked because in all their years together, he only had one losing season.

As the years went by, Ed's friends told him time and time again, "Thomas, you found the only woman in the world who would put up with you." Ed was many things, but he was not the least bit handy. He once had to call and ask a friend how to get a bottle of Windex to work. He could dissect a 4-3 defense, but he had no idea how to fix the lawn mower or the garbage disposal or do any of the normal "honey do" projects that husbands take care of around the house. Nor did he have the patience to manage the household finances. On top of that, he worked a lot of hours, especially during football season. After he became athletic director, his sports season never ended.

So from the beginning of their marriage Jan took care of almost everything at home. She balanced the checkbook, changed the light-bulbs, painted the walls, cleaned the gutters, and kept the house and the household in order. And she was OK with that. From the time they first dated, Ed told her how he believed God had called him to be a teacher and coach. The school was his mission field. Jan shared that calling, and by taking on more and more of the household responsibilities, she made it possible for Ed to spend more time with his players and students. If his focus had been purely on football and winning games, she never would have gone for this arrange-ment. However, she knew Ed's calling went far beyond the football field. She, too, wanted to make an eternal difference in the lives of his players, and the best way she could do that was to be the source of refuge and the encouragement Ed needed to keep going. With every bad loss, he came home depressed, ready to quit. She listened and tried to encourage him. Yet more than once she said, "You've lived with this loss long enough. It's time to get up and get going." He listened and did exactly what she said.

And Ed encouraged Jan to pursue her own interests. When their sons were in grade school, she decided she wanted to go through EMT training and become a paramedic. "You will be great at it," Ed said. He responded the same way when she decided to take a job outside the home. They had the kind of relationship where they could each pursue their interests without the other feeling threat-ened by it. All the while, both of them worked hard at their jobs during the day and made time for long walks with each other in the evenings. Somehow, Ed usually found a way to make sure those walks ended up at the local ice cream place.

Neither gave a lot of thought to the way in which they had arranged their household responsibilities. It was what it was. Jan took care of things at home, while Ed took care of things at school. Shortly after the tornado, that arrangement unraveled. When their house blew away, Jan naturally took charge of making sure it was rebuilt. She found an apartment for them to stay in while the work was being done and picked out their new cars, including a little red truck for Ed. At the same time, she put their finances back in order, chased down all the missing bills, and settled with the insurance adjusters. She hired the contractor that Todd recommended, without competing bids, and watched over the rebuilding of their house on a daily basis. In addition, as assistant city clerk, she did the same things for the town of Parkersburg, only on a larger scale.

Ed, meanwhile, juggled meetings with insurance adjusters and contractors at the school along with overseeing the rebuilding of the athletic fields. He sat in on meetings with the superintendent and principal in which they planned the design for the new school, as well as plotting the logistics of the upcoming new school year. They had to figure out a way to move 225 high school students into the middle school without moving the middle school students. He also taught summer driver's education classes, which started two days after the tornado. Neither Ed nor Jan had a moment to call their own, and both found themselves so tired at the end of the day that they barely had enough strength to eat a quick meal and head to bed.

After church one Sunday, Jan overheard a friend ask Ed, "Have things settled down for you yet? Has it gotten any easier now that you have a place to stay and your house is going back up?"

Ed said something he did not realize he would soon regret. "I think it has somewhat for Jan," he said.

When she heard those words come out of his mouth, Jan nearly exploded. *What are you smoking?* she wanted to say. Before that moment, she didn't realize how much she resented the fact that Ed had thrown all of their home responsibilities on her after the tornado. She also did not appreciate his lack of acknowledgment of the heavy responsibilities she carried with the city, especially now. Again, she had never really formulated these feelings into concrete thoughts; instead they sat below the surface. As soon as she heard Ed's words to their friend, her anger came rushing to the surface. She nearly jumped on him right then. Throughout their marriage she had never been shy about expressing her feelings. However, she knew she needed to take a moment to cool off to keep from saying anything she might want to take back later.

Ed noticed the smoke coming out of Jan's ears. He started to say something but thought better of it. Later that afternoon, he pulled her aside and said, "We need to talk." He, too, had felt the distance growing between them, and he did not like it.

Over the next couple of hours in their small apartment above True Value Hardware in downtown Parkersburg, the two of them got brutally honest with one another. They realized they had allowed their work lives to become so all-consuming that they were nothing more than ships passing in the night. The two slept in the same apartment but were so exhausted that they never interacted. "That's not the kind of relationship I want," Jan said.

"Neither do I," Ed said. "So what do we need to do to fix it?"

Ed and Jan's relationship changed after that Sunday afternoon conversation. The two worked at becoming more sensitive to what the other was going through in their jobs. They worked at helping and supporting one another. Both realized that they were in danger of letting the aftermath of the storm pull them apart. Yet, in truth, they now understood that over the years they had let their work lives encroach far too much into their life together. Ed did not all of a sudden turn into a handyman after that discussion, and the only part of their house he actually picked out was the 46-inch Sony flat screen television, but he did spend much more time at the house working on the cleanup and doing whatever he could around the house. Jan went to the school more often to check on the progress being made there.

More than anything, the two of them took the time to remember why they had fallen in love with each other in the first place. For months after the tornado, Ed and Jan found themselves living in the kind of apartment that newlyweds without a penny to their name usually rent. Looking back, they found it oddly appropriate, for this was a fresh start for more than the football team and the town; it was a fresh start for the Thomases as well.

CHAPTER 6

UNPARALLELED OPPORTUNITY

If all I have taught you is how to block and tackle,
then I have failed you as a coach.
ED THOMAS

THE A-P FOOTBALL TEAM DRIFTED INTO THE ELEMENTARY school cafeteria for a team meeting two days after the tornado struck. The Parkersburg half of the team flashed back to sitting in this room, eating peanut butter and jelly sandwiches while talking about their flag football teams and dreaming of the day they would get to be real A-P Falcons. To those from Aplington, it was just another school cafeteria.

Several of the Parkersburg players were in the same boat as assistant coach Jon Wiegmann and his son, defensive back Coy. Jon had been out of town on the day of the tornado, but Coy and two other starters from the A-P football team, Jimmy Clark and Alex Hornbuckle, were hanging out in the Wiegmanns' backyard. When the sirens went off, they ran to Coy's bedroom, which also happened to be in the basement of the family home. His mother and sister were already there. Once the storm passed, the five were surprised to find that the house was relatively intact, although it was in a different place than it had been when they went down into

75

the basement. The tornado had picked up the house and dropped it back down askew on its foundation in one heavily damaged piece. The house on their right appeared to be directly in the storm's path, yet it was unharmed. The house on the left, which should have been safe, was completely destroyed.

Compared to several of his teammates, Coy was lucky. Many players lost their homes and everything they called their own. Their lives were scattered across town, but they still came to the team meeting.

Coach Thomas may have called the meeting, but the seniors on the team made it happen. As soon as Coach said he wanted to talk to the team, they phoned or sent text messages to all the other players. That spring, not long before the tornado, Coach held a draft, where every senior selected five underclassmen for whom they were responsible during summer lifting and workouts, as well as during the season. The system worked, because every player who hoped to suit up for the 2008 A-P football team was in the elementary school cafeteria, sitting quietly when Coach Ed Thomas walked in the room.

"Fellas, I really appreciate you making the effort to come over here this morning," Coach began. "I know some of you lost your homes on Sunday, and I want to tell you how sorry I am that this has happened. You young people whose homes were hit have a lot of work ahead of you, so I won't take up too much time. But I wanted to meet with you face-to-face and tell you myself that . . . ," Ed paused and cleared his throat, trying to keep his composure. "I wanted to tell you myself that, God willing, we will play our first home game against West Marshall on our own field on September 5."

The moment he spoke those words, players jumped up and started high-fiving one another. A smile broke out on every face.

"Now, you need to understand that we're not doing this for us; we're doing this for our entire town, for the community. And I'm so proud of you fellas for the way that you've already been out there, working, helping people. Every time I turn around, I see you out there, digging people out, manning chain saws, dragging rubble and furniture out and helping people get to their belongings. I can't tell you how proud that makes me to see you like that.

"I don't know if you realize it or not, but you've got a tremendous experience ahead of you here. Because of this tornado, you now have the opportunity to show the kind of character we're made of. You know, adversity is a test of character. It shows what's already inside you. But it also shapes character, and I believe that is already happening with you fellas. I've watched you working side by side, helping people with no hidden agendas, doing it because it is the right thing to do. When you do the right thing, good things happen. You are going to see that this is even more true right now with what we're going through as a team as a result of this tornado.

"We've got a lot of work ahead of us, but as the juniors and seniors will tell the rest of ya, this team is built on hard work. When we work hard, and we work together, we will be successful. And the most important work we can do is helping others. Real success is measured not by how much money you have or how many games we win, but by the impact you make on others during your lifetimes. You have an opportunity to impact a lot of lives and help a lot of people in this town. It's right in front of you. You just have to take hold of it.

"Well, fellas, that's all I have. Thanks for coming, and let's get to work." With that, Ed walked out.

Senior Alec Thompson stood up. Two days earlier, Alec and his father, superintendent Jon Thompson, had stood outside their Aplington home, watching the sky for the storms the weathermen warned were on their way. They watched a mass of clouds begin swirling together, forming the funnel cloud that became the EF5 tornado. The funnel cloud passed directly over their home. As it moved toward the east, the cloud transformed into a massive wall of black, headed straight for Parkersburg. Alec was the first player to arrive at the school after the tornado. He had spent the past two days cutting up trees, dragging debris, and digging people out of their homes all across the south side of Parkersburg. Almost every player in the room had done the same thing.

"Hey, guys," Alec said, "we're going to move all the equipment out of the weight room over to the middle school in Aplington. Coach said he wanted to get it someplace dry. We also need some guys to get our helmets and pads and jerseys out of the locker room and bring them over here. The locker room is the only room in the whole school that didn't collapse, so we should be able to salvage about everything."

With that, the players took off. Those who didn't move equipment fanned out across the football, baseball, and softball fields, picking up shredded hunks of plywood, pulling two-by-fours out of the turf, and clearing the fields of all the large pieces of debris. Other students joined them as they rescued most of the books from the school library, along with all the athletic trophies and everything else they could save from inside the school. Periodically, one of the assistant coaches came by and sent a group of students to a house where people needed help. This same scene played out every day for weeks.

On the Wednesday after the tornado, Ed made a strange request to a group of players helping him take down a mangled chain-link fence at the far side of the field. "Hey, guys, my wife asked me if any of you would be willing to help out the town. The city workers usually dig the graves over at the cemetery, but they are all tied up trying to get power poles back up and things like that. We may need about six of you to go over and dig a couple of graves for some of the people who died on Sunday."

Coy Wiegmann was one of the six players working with the coach right then. To Coy, Coach didn't even need to ask. All he had to do was point in the right direction, and he was there. Coy had never dug a grave before, but that didn't matter. The next day Al Kerns, one of the assistant coaches, walked over and told Coy, "Yep, they need you guys." Several hours later, Coy, Alex Hornbuckle, Curry Hoff, and Spencer Cooper crawled out of a double-sized grave.* The next day they were back at the school with the same question: "What do you need us to do next?"

Television crews descended on Parkersburg, turning the high school and the south end of town into a media circus. Television news vans from Cedar Falls, Waterloo, and Des Moines covered one part of the school parking lot, their antennas fully extended. Cameramen trailed behind reporters, most of whom, it seemed, chased Coach Thomas. "You know who you ought to be talking to," Coach said after his umpteenth interview. "You should go talk to these young people. They're the ones who headed up this whole cleanup operation."

"Which one should we talk to?" a reporter yelled back.

"All of them," Coach said.†

✦ ✦ ✦

Since Ed Thomas first arrived in the town of Parkersburg his teams had always reflected his core values of hard work, sacrifice, and commitment on the field. Yet Ed made it clear that these lessons were about far more than football. He told every team he coached, "If all I have taught you is how to block and tackle, then I have failed you as a coach." Now, more than ever before, his team showed the full impact of his words and example. Ed didn't have to ask his players to come to the school to help move books from the library and the weight-lifting equipment from the weight room. They came on their own, and they came to work wherever they were needed. Ed chalked this up to the Iowa work ethic and community spirit. For his players it was something more. Sure, they came because of their concern for their community, but they also came and worked because they knew this is what Coach Thomas

---

*For video of the players digging the graves, go to *www.youtube.com/watch?v=z2Cj08vktG4&feature=related.*

†For raw video of interviews with Coach Thomas, go to *www.youtube.com/watch?v=s3Lq95Kg9Ug.*

wanted and expected from them. And to a man, none of them wanted to let him down.

Ed understood how they felt. He had had the same relationship with his high school football coach. With his father being largely absent during his high school years, Ed found a strong role model in Coach Jerry Dawley. Ed caught the coach's eye on the first day of practice when he showed up in better condition as a freshman than anyone else on the team. Back in those days, football teams did not have off-season conditioning programs. But Ed did. At least a month before the first two-a-day practices, he started running laps at the local horse track. When other players collapsed after endless rounds of wind sprints, Ed kept going. Coaches notice things like that.

Coach Dawley soon found Ed had an inexhaustible appetite for everything football. Ed's mother prayed he would become a preacher, but Ed always seemed destined to be a coach, from organizing pickup games in his neighborhood to drawing up football plays like other kids doodled. Once he started playing for Jerry Dawley, he saw the real impact a coach can make. Coach Dawley gave Ed an amazing gift. He made Ed believe that he could accomplish anything he put his mind to if he was willing to work hard enough to make it happen.

By his junior year, Ed was Coach Dawley's starting quarterback. Dawley even let Ed call his own plays, something Ed never did with his own quarterbacks—not even for his own sons. It was like Dawley had another coach on the field. Perhaps that is why he never let anyone lay a hand on Ed during practices. That didn't exactly endear Ed to his teammates who played defense, but they got over that frustration once they left the football field. Even in high school, Ed's peers respected him because he lived with passion what he believed. When his sister Susan ran for FFA sweetheart, he voted for the other girl, lest anyone think he played favorites.

By the time he graduated from high school, Ed knew he wanted to become a high school football coach. He wanted to make the same kind of difference in the lives of young men that Coach Dawley made in his.

And he did make a difference. You could see it all over town, even in the most unlikely places.

◆ ◆ ◆

One night, Ed and his assistant coaches walked into Tooters Bar and Grill in Parkersburg, which also happened to serve the best pizza in town. Al Kerns, Ed's longtime defensive coordinator, walked in first. He glanced over at the bar and noticed three former Falcon players sitting at the bar, a beer and a cigarette in front of each. By the time Coach Thomas walked in the door, the beers and cigarettes had disappeared. Al laughed and shook his head. More than a dozen years had passed since any of these guys had played for Coach, yet they cared about what he thought of them.

Rusty Eddy was one of those former players in the pizza place that night. Rusty dreamed of playing for Coach Thomas from the time he was in first grade. His dream turned into a nightmare during the first two-a-day practice of his freshman year of high school. About halfway through the second practice of the day, he wanted to go up to Coach and tell him, "Excuse me, but I thought I had signed up to play football, not enlist in the Marine Corps." But he didn't. He kept his mouth shut as he ran wind sprints and went through blocking drills and ran something the coach called "gut busters" and ran and ran and ran some more. Even when practice was over, the team had to run off the field and into the locker room.

As soon as practice was over, Rusty walked to the local convenience store and bought a thirty-two ounce bottle of Pepsi and a salted nut roll. Both were gone before he completed the short walk to his house.

Once home, he collapsed on the sofa, looked at his father, and said, "Dad, I want to quit football."

"No problem. You can quit as soon as the season is over."

"What? That's not quitting. That's just not going out for the team as a sophomore."

"Well," his dad said, "that's quitting to me."

Rusty didn't argue. He slumped off to his room, where he soaked his aching feet in Epsom salts before going to bed. The next morning he went back to practice. And the next. And the next. Once school started, the team only practiced once a day. That didn't make things much better for Rusty. He had study hall at the end of the day, but he couldn't study. Instead he sat and dreaded practice. Once it started, he didn't feel any better. Over and over he asked himself, "What's the point of working this hard to play a game?" He never came up with a good answer, at least not while in high school.

Rusty never started a game as a freshman. In fact, over the course of his high school playing career, he only started one game, and that came during his senior year. Even then, he started against the worst team in the conference. Rusty wasn't what one might call athletically gifted in high school. However, he never quit football. When it came time for two-a-days a couple of weeks before school started for his sophomore year, he was there. And the next year, and the next. He still didn't like football any more than he did as a freshman, but he could not walk away from Coach Thomas. Quitting the team would let his coach down, and that's something Rusty could not do, not even after breaking his hand during practice as a freshman. Rusty never quit, and Coach Thomas never quit on him.

Coach had reason to quit on Rusty. During his junior year, Rusty and his friends decided to break into the school after a night of drinking. They didn't do anything malicious. Instead, they went to the gym, where they threw the large, foam, pole-vault landing pads into a pile. When the police arrived, Rusty and his buddies were diving off the bleachers onto the pads. No charges were filed, but he was suspended from school for three days. Not long after that, he was suspended again for skipping school, and then a third time for getting into trouble for doing something stupid. Even so, he had the good sense not to get himself suspended during football season. He may have spent most of his football career riding the bench, but he still didn't want to do anything to jeopardize his spot on the team.

Each time Rusty found himself suspended, a visitor came to his house to talk to him about the choices he kept on making. That visitor was, of course, the one man he did not want to disappoint—Coach Thomas. Like Coach's father, Rusty's dad was an alcoholic and his mother a teetotaler. His parents tried to hold the family together as long as they could, but eventually Rusty's dad moved out, and the marriage ended. Coach Thomas filled the void for Rusty. Ed didn't treat him any differently than he did any other player, but Rusty saw in him the man he hoped to become. Like a father, Coach constantly pushed Rusty, yelling at him during practice, "Come on, Falcon, push yourself; get the lead out!" and then patting him on the back and telling him what a great job he had just done on a block or a tackle.

That is why when Rusty found himself in trouble, Ed was there. "You can do better than this, Rusty," Ed said. "I know you can. You can do anything you set your mind to doing. But not like this. Not with these choices. You can do better." When Ed came by his house, Ed never said anything to Rusty that he didn't say to the entire team during practice, but somehow it had a lot more impact coming from him one-on-one.

Early on a Friday morning toward the end of his junior year, Rusty awoke to the sound of a woman calling his name. He got up, walked to the stairway, and looked down to see one of his mother's closest friends standing at the bottom of the stairs. "Rusty," she said, "your father died last night. He killed himself." She didn't elaborate. As soon as she told him the news, she turned and walked away. Rusty could hear his mother sobbing at the kitchen table.

Rusty stumbled back into his room and collapsed on his bed, numb from head to toe. A few minutes later, he heard another voice—that of Coach Ed Thomas. There was no mistaking that voice.

Ed came up to his room and sat down on the bed next to him. The two of them sat in silence for a few minutes, staring off in the same direction. Tears welled up in Ed's eyes as he fought to hold himself together. Finally he said, "Rus, I'm sorry to hear about your dad. From what I hear, he was a good person and had a lot of friends around him. I wish you didn't have to go through this, and I wish there was something I could say to make you feel better. When you need me, I'll always be here for you and your brother. I love ya." Rusty was all of sixteen years old.

Ed was right about Rusty. His life turned out dramatically different from his father's. Today he is a social worker and counselor, working to make a difference in the lives of others. A lot of factors contributed to Rusty's turnaround, not the least of which was a high school football coach who believed Rusty was more than the son of an alcoholic, the product of a broken home, and a survivor of a parent's suicide. Coach saw potential in Rusty Eddy and refused to give up on him, even when Rusty wanted to give up on himself.

In his thirty-four years of coaching, Ed worked with a lot of Rustys—kids who provided the reason he was there, being a coach, a teacher, a counselor, a father figure, just as his high school coach had been all of those things for him.

CHAPTER 7

"YOU WOULD DO THE SAME THING FOR ME"

We never talk about winning to our players.
We talk about doing the little things correctly,
about doing what is right,
about being first-class on and off the field.
ED THOMAS

ED KNEW THEY WERE COMING, BUT THAT DIDN'T PREPARE him for the emotions that swept over him as he watched the two school buses pull into the parking lot of the Methodist church that overlooked Ed Thomas Field. "Two buses," he said to anyone who happened to be nearby. "Wow, two entire buses." Tears welled up in his eyes at the sight of the long line of students filing off the buses, one after the other. When road teams came to Parkersburg, Ed always looked at the visitors' side of the field and said, "Hmm, I thought they'd bring more." He didn't think that on this day. The line of high school students made their way down from the church to the football field. At the end of the line came Coach Tom Wilson of Dowling High School in West Des Moines, over one hundred miles away.

Tom and Ed had a long history together. Tom coached high

school football in Iowa for five years before taking a graduate assistant position at Ball State University in Muncie, Indiana. A few years later, he decided to return to Iowa. Three high schools offered him jobs. Tom chose Dike-New Hartford High School, twelve miles straight east of Parkersburg. At the time he knew Ed Thomas only by reputation, but he chose that particular job because of him. Tom always said that to be the best, you have to beat the best. What better place to measure himself in than by taking a job where he had to play Parkersburg every year?

Up until that time, Dike-New Hartford's football program resembled Parkersburg's before Ed arrived. In the twelve years since Dike and New Hartford consolidated, they had yet to have a winning season. Worst of all, they lost nearly every year to A-P, and the people in both Dike and New Hartford were sick and tired of it. When Tom interviewed for the job, all the superintendent, principal, and athletic director talked about was beating Ed Thomas and Aplington-Parkersburg. Tom thought they needed to learn how to beat *anyone* before they worried about beating one of the best teams in the state. Because the two schools were so close together, Dike-New Hartford and A-P should have been fierce rivals, but A-P so dominated the series that the rivalry only went one way.

All that changed during Tom's second season. Dike-New Hartford came into Parkersburg and beat A-P on its home field. At long last, a rivalry was born. Over Tom's next eight seasons, the Dike-New Hartford versus Aplington-Parkersburg game became one of the most competitive and hardest-fought games of the year for both schools. Most years, both teams came in ranked at or near the top of their respective divisions. While fierce rivals on the field, Tom and Ed became close friends. Each had the utmost respect for the other. Ed admired the way in which Tom prepared his teams and the amazing turnaround he brought to Dike. Tom looked at Ed as the standard by which he measured his own coaching career, not just in terms of wins and losses, but by the integrity and class Ed displayed in everything he did.

Tom heard a lot of coaches talking about how faith should come before football, but for most it was only that—talk. Tom watched Ed closely. He knew Ed was a Christian—Ed never kept that a secret. Yet Tom, along with everyone else who knew Ed, marveled at how Ed never shoved Jesus down anyone's throat. Ed saved his sermons for the occasional times he filled in for his pastor at his church. Instead, Ed's life was his sermon. Saint Francis of Assisi once said, "Preach the gospel at all times. If necessary, use words." If Saint Francis had lived in northeastern Iowa, no doubt he would have had Ed Thomas in mind when he said this.

Tom Wilson and Ed remained friends after Tom left Dike-New Hartford to move to a larger school in West Des Moines. He even sought Ed's advice when considering his new position. A lot of coaches throughout Iowa sought Ed's advice on a regular basis. Although Ed and Tom did not play against each other any longer, they kept in touch.

The moment Tom heard the news about the tornado, he knew what he wanted to do. He called Ed and told him he planned on bringing some students to help with the cleanup. He then sent out e-mails to parents and had an announcement made at school during the last two days of classes. Ninety-six students signed up to go to Parkersburg and help. The students laughed and talked throughout the two-hour bus ride. However, the moment they topped the hill on Highway 14 and saw the destruction, they grew silent.

Tom followed his students over to Ed Thomas Field. About a quarter of the way across the field, he came face-to-face with its namesake. Ed bit hard on his lip and shook his head, fighting to control his emotions. He grabbed Tom's hand and put his other hand on his friend's shoulder. "I can't tell you how much this means to me, Tom." Ed paused and looked down for a moment. His voice cracked. "Thank you for coming."

"Coach, I know you would do the same thing for me," Tom replied. "Now what do you want us to do?"

Ed stepped back and looked over the field. "We've picked up

all the big stuff off the field, but it is still a mess. There are nails and glass and everything else you can imagine driven down into the turf. Let's get your kids down here and put them on it. They'll have to crawl on their hands and knees to do it; some of the debris is driven down really deep." He looked Tom in the eye and broke out into a grin. "You know, Tom, there's no one I can think of that I would rather have down on their hands and knees on my field than you."

"Well, don't get used to it," Tom said and slapped Ed on the back. He then started barking out orders to the students. Tom had his students line up side by side and slowly work their way across the field. Once they worked their way across, they went back over it, then over it again. In all, the Dowling students spent six hours combing through the grass of the field, pulling out every last nail and shard of glass.

A few minutes after Tom and his students arrived, Ed's cell phone rang. Up until his landline phone blew away with his house, Ed refused to get a cell phone. However, after the storm, so many reporters, contractors, and well-wishers called the school administration building that secretaries hardly had time to get anything done. Finally, the school superintendent had enough. He drove over to the football field, found Ed, and slapped a cell phone in his hand. "It's time you enter the twenty-first century, Ed," he said. Four days later, Ed had the hang of it. He answered his phone and talked for a few moments. Then he handed the phone to Tom Wilson, who was standing next to him. "Here. Peter King of *Sports Illustrated* wants to talk to you."

"What? Why?" Tom said. He couldn't understand why one of the most popular writers from the top sports magazine in the country would want to talk to him.

"He's writing something about the tornado relief efforts. I told him you brought some students over, and now he wants to talk to you."

Tom shook his head and rolled his eyes. He took the phone,

gathered himself for a moment, and said, "Hello." After talking to King, he handed the phone back to Ed. "I don't see what the big deal is," Tom said. "What were we supposed to do? Sit at home in Des Moines and pretend we didn't know you? Like I said, you would do the same thing for me."

Two other teachers came over from Dowling with the students. Tom put them in charge of clearing the field and then asked Ed, "How is Teep doing?" Teep was Tom Teeple, a fixture on the sidelines at every A-P home football game. Ed and Teep had been friends since the day over thirty-five years earlier when Teep and Sue moved from Parkersburg to What Cheer, Ed's hometown. Teep had pulled his moving truck into the local gas station, when an eighteen-year-old kid with hair down over his ears and wearing a blue leisure suit looked up from the paper he was reading and yelled out, "So who are you?" Teep told him who he was, then asked the kid who he was. "I'm Ed Thomas, and this is my hometown. I go to college over at William Penn." The two hit if off immediately. They were close in age and shared a love for sports. While Ed was in college, they played softball and basketball together. Not long after Ed moved to Parkersburg, Teeple moved back to town and bought out the local barber. He soon became one of Parkersburg High School's biggest supporters. That is how Tom Wilson got to know him. Teep worked the first-down chains and spent a lot of time standing next to the opposing team's coaches. He and Coach Wilson hit it off from the start.

"We nearly lost him," Ed told Tom Wilson. "You know Sue is in a wheelchair because of her MS. When the sirens went off, Teep tried to take cover, but he couldn't get her in the basement. He pushed her chair onto a landing near one corner of their kitchen, covered her with a blanket, and held on for dear life. When the tornado hit their house, he held on to her as best he could. He said the wind straightened him out like Superman before it finally sucked him halfway out of his house."

"My gosh, how bad was he hurt?"

"A few cuts and bruises, but other than that, he was fine. Sue came through untouched. Rescuers found her under the blanket in that corner."

"All right, I've got to go see him," Tom said.

When they arrived at what once was the Teeple house, they found Teep working away, sorting through rubble. Tom and Ed, along with a handful of students, jumped in and helped Teep the best they could.

Tom Wilson was the first coach to bring a busload of students to Parkersburg, but he was far from the last. Dike-New Hartford brought a group, as did West Marshall and most of the other schools A-P played every season. University of Iowa coach Kirk Ferentz brought sixty players over later in June. Ferentz shared a special bond with Coach Thomas. Three former A-P players had suited up at the University of Iowa and gone on to play in the National Football League. Through these three players, Ferentz saw firsthand the fruit of the A-P way. Yet that wasn't what endeared Ed Thomas to him. Ferentz's first few teams after he came to the University of Iowa struggled. In his first two seasons he won all of four games while losing nineteen. Yet during those losing seasons, he received regular letters and calls from Ed, encouraging him to hang in there. A lot of people called when the Hawkeyes did well, but Ed was one of the few who called when Ferentz's team was down, and he never forgot that.

Other coaches throughout the state brought students to Parkersburg or sent letters of encouragement to Ed. They did it out of their respect for him. Every coach in the state of Iowa, and those around the country who knew Ed, pointed to the class and character he displayed on and off the field as the reason they brought busloads of students to Parkersburg.

Fellow coaches and their teams were not the only ones who rushed to Parkersburg to help. Green Bay Packers defensive end Aaron Kampman and his wife, Linde, were in Kansas City, visiting family the day the tornado struck Parkersburg. Aaron had just completed his most successful season as a pro, being named a starter for the National Football Conference in the 2008 Pro Bowl ten years after graduating from A-P. Aaron showed his appreciation to his coach by giving him his jersey from the Pro Bowl, which Ed proudly displayed in his classroom.

When he heard the news of the tornado, Aaron called his coaches in Green Bay and told them he would be a little late for the minicamp scheduled to begin that week. By 4:30 on Monday morning, May 26, he and his brother-in-law were in Aaron's car, headed to Parkersburg. Along the way they stopped and bought chain saws, work gloves, boots, and anything else they might need. Aaron grew up in Aplington, but his wife's parents lived near the Thomases' home in Parkersburg, as did Aaron's grandfather. His grandfather went down into his basement when the sirens went off. He thought the storm had passed and went upstairs to see what was left of his house. He left the basement too early. The tornado carried off his house — with him in it. He woke up in the hospital, and the first words out of his mouth were "God is so good to me."

Word of his grandfather's injuries had not yet reached Aaron when he drove into town. "It looks like someone threw the entire town into a blender," he said to his brother-in-law. He was headed to his grandfather's house when he turned a corner. Ed and Jan were right in front of him, digging through the rubble of their house. Aaron jumped out of his car and started walking toward his old high school coach. Ed turned and saw him. The tears started once more. Aaron gave his coach a huge hug and told him, "Coach, everything will be OK." Aaron spent that day and the next in town, cutting up fallen trees and hauling brush away.

Former A-P offensive lineman Casey Wiegmann* had just signed with the Denver Broncos and could not leave their mandatory off-season workouts when the tornado struck. However, at

---

*No relation to assistant coach Jon Wiegmann or to A-P starting center Mike Wiegmann.

the end of practice on the day after the storm, head coach Mike Shanahan called the entire team together. He explained what had happened to Casey's hometown. "Casey's high school was wiped out," the coach said, "and they need a lot of help rebuilding it. The NFL has a program where they will match anything you choose to donate. You guys can do whatever you want, but I'm giving the first $5,000." As soon as the mandatory practices were over, Casey went back to Parkersburg, as did the other two NFL players from A-P—Jared Devries of the Detroit Lions and Brad Meester of the Jacksonville Jaguars.

Over the next several weeks, all four NFL players not only helped with cleanup in town; they helped organize fund-raising operations that raised $250,000 to rebuild the school, not just the football field. All four still had family in the area, but there was something more that motivated them to go beyond writing a check to the relief efforts. "I remember something my high school football coach, Ed Thomas, said to me when I left home," Kampman told *Sports Illustrated*'s Peter King. "Never forget where you come from. Being from here, you can't forget." Wiegmann added, "Ed Thomas was like a second father to me."

Tom Wilson spoke for everyone—coaches, players, and friends alike—when he told Ed, "You would do the same thing for me." In many ways, he already had.

CHAPTER 8

AFTER THE CAMERAS DISAPPEAR

Take pride in what you do.
ED THOMAS

THE ALARM WENT OFF, AND ED CLIMBED OUT OF BED. LIGHT had not yet filtered through the windows of the small apartment above True Value Hardware. He stumbled over to his dresser, dug out his clothes for the day, and headed off for the shower

By the time Ed came out of the bathroom, Jan was up. They exchanged a quick kiss. "What's on your agenda today?" Ed asked.

"Pretty much the same as yesterday. You?"

"The same. Weight room at Tuve's. Driver's ed. Then it's back to the school and the contractors and volunteers. Just like every day."

"We'll get our lives back eventually," Jan said.

"I guess so, but sometimes it sure doesn't feel like it," Ed said.

Jan then headed to the shower while Ed sat at the kitchen table with his Bible, just as he had every day since he was a boy reading through the Bible with his grandmother. That summer he was spending most of his time in one of his favorite books of the Bible, the Psalms. The writers, especially David, focused on God's faithfulness, even in times of difficulty. Ed needed that reassurance, especially now. So did Jan. She spent most of that summer in one chapter of the Bible: Psalm 121. She recited the first two verses daily, if not minute by minute: "I lift up my eyes to the hills—where does my help come from? My help comes from the LORD, the Maker of heaven and earth."

Before Jan came out of the shower, Ed was already off to the makeshift weight room at John Tuve's house north of town. Even though the high school was gone, Ed didn't see any reason to cancel his off-season conditioning program. During the team's spring meeting a few weeks before the tornado, he handed out the schedule for the "voluntary" lifting and running program that started as soon as school ended. A little thing like a tornado wasn't going to get him off schedule.

Ed arrived at the Tuves' horse barn/football weight room at 5:30 a.m. A handful of players were already there, even though the first of two morning lifting sessions didn't begin until 6:00. Ed unlocked the doors of the arena and flipped on the lights. "OK, fellas, let's get started," Ed told the players who drifted in the door. Over the next hour, he demonstrated the proper way to do squats to one player, cheered another on as he pushed himself toward a personal best in the bench press, and ribbed another about his new girlfriend.

A few minutes before 7:00, Al Kerns came in and took over. Ed dashed over to the grade school parking lot for the start of his driver's ed class. Only two of the three students who were supposed to drive that day had arrived. Coy Wiegmann, Ed's backup quarterback and starting defensive back, was a little late, but only because he had to finish his reps at the weight room on the Tuves' farm. Once Coy arrived, Ed settled into the passenger seat and said to the student behind the wheel, "Take a right out of the parking lot and go straight down Highway 57." He then turned on the radio, which he had set on his favorite country music station, and settled back for the ride. When they came to the stop sign on the eastern edge of town where they often turned south to go to Highway 20, a four-lane divided highway, to practice freeway driving, Ed said,

"Keep going straight." Eventually he had the driver turn north just outside of Cedar Falls, then back to the east a little while later.

Eventually they ended up in Denver, Iowa. "Pull in here," Ed said as they came to Denver High School. The student parked the car next to the football field. Ed got out and went onto the field. He walked around on the grass for a while, looking it over like an appraiser on *Antiques Roadshow* inspecting a Ming vase. "You can tell a lot about a football program by the way they take care of their field," he said. The other student took the wheel, and they headed back to Parkersburg by way of Dike, Iowa, where Ed had another field to inspect.

About the time Ed arrived at the grade school to start driver's ed, Jan was finishing her breakfast at Dutch's, a local diner, with her neighbor and a small group of regulars. The neighbor was also living in an apartment above True Value Hardware. In fact, she had told Jan about the apartments the night after the tornado when they drove over to Cedar Falls together to buy toothbrushes and other basics they needed right after the storm. They moved into their apartments on the same day.

After a quick breakfast, Jan shot over to the house. Aaron and Todd had spent most of the previous day separating wood debris from metal so that it could be carted off. Most of the pad had been cleared, and construction was already under way. However, the task of digging through and carting away rubble never seemed to end. Given Ed's and Jan's schedules, debris clearing fell to Aaron and Todd, although they didn't have much more time for it than did their parents. Even though Aaron had the summer off from teaching, he ran a corn detasseling crew through the summer. Todd's days were filled with his work as a financial planner. On top of that, he and Candice were trying to finalize details of their upcoming wedding. Even so, Aaron and Todd did as much as they could. Later, as construction kicked into high gear, Todd stayed in constant contact by phone with the contractor.

On this morning, and every morning, Jan came by the house to check everything out before heading to work. She would be back that evening when she finally pulled herself away from the building that was housing the temporary city hall. Then it would be off to Cedar Falls to select fixtures, carpet, and furniture. Something always had to be picked out, which made this a nearly daily task for Jan.

After finishing his morning drive time with his students, Ed darted into Dutch's for a quick bite to eat before heading over to the high school. On his way, he pulled out his phone to make a call. "Hey, just checking in. How is your morning going?" he said to Jan. He called her every day at this same time. Since their conversation that Sunday afternoon, Ed made sure he and Jan talked several times during the day, even though the temporary insanity of the summer meant that neither of them had any time to call their own. They talked again by phone during lunch and again when Jan got off work. Once their home, the school, and the city hall were back in working order, they would get back to their evening walks around town. For now, quick phone calls throughout the day would have to do.

Once he arrived at the high school, Ed went straight to his "office." Shortly after the tornado cleanup began, he found a teacher's desk in one of the classrooms and dragged it out onto the hill overlooking the football field. That's where he set up shop every morning. He pulled a large, folded-up sheet of paper out of his back pocket, smoothed it out on his desk, and got busy. That piece of paper contained the name and number of every contractor working on the athletic fields, as well as the names and contact information of his legion of volunteers. The giant piece of paper also contained a schedule of what he needed to accomplish each day.

And he had a lot to accomplish every day.

Every athletic facility at the school had to be replaced. Every single one. Obviously, the gym was gone, and so was the football field. But the baseball and softball fields had also sustained heavy damage. That presented a huge problem for Ed as athletic director, because in Iowa, high school baseball and softball start their seasons about the time school lets out. Within a day or two of the tornado, Ed and the baseball and softball coaches held a meeting in Ed's outdoor office to plot out revised schedules for each team, along with finding a place for A-P's home games. In addition, the girls' volleyball team's practices started in early August, with their season beginning when the boy's football season began. Ed had to find a gym for their home games, along with a place for them to practice.

Then there was football. Truth be told, time was already running low when Ed boldly declared that A-P would begin their season at home right on schedule. Playing a home game meant more than clearing the rubble off the field. Huge hunks of turf had been torn out. In addition to the gashes, the ground was uneven from the combination of heavy rain, foot traffic, and large chunks of houses that had fallen out of the sky on top of it. A turf specialist from Iowa State University came over and helped rehabilitate the playing surface.

But the team needed more than a field on which to play their game. Everything around Ed Thomas Field had been heavily damaged. The bleachers on the home side of the field had to be torn down. Every one of the long metal benches that served as the seats first had to be removed so that the structure underneath could be razed. All of the lights—poles and all—had to be replaced, and the track surrounding the field had to be scraped up and resurfaced. The press box was gone, as was the scoreboard. As if that weren't enough, all of the concession stands, ticket booths, bathrooms, and everything else that made Friday night football games possible had to be rebuilt from the ground up. Throughout the summer, Ed had an army of school coworkers, volunteers, and contractors to help with the rebuilding efforts. Every day, parents and students showed up and asked one question: What can we do to help?

Ed's first team captain, Dave Becker, spent nearly as much time at the football field as he did at home that summer. Dave wasn't just a former player who wanted to help out his old coach. His youngest son, Scott, was a junior on the team. Dave, like most of the rest of the team parents, knew how much the team and its coach meant to his son. He wanted to see the team play its first game at home nearly as much as Ed did.

All three of Dave and Joan's sons played football for Ed. Their oldest, Brad, only played one season, in 1998. That also happened to be Todd Thomas's senior year. Scott, the youngest, was about to play his third season for Ed. And Mark, their middle son, played for four years for A-P, including the state championship team of 2001. The fact that Mark was able to be a part of that team made Coach Thomas very special to Dave Becker. Mark got into trouble during his freshman year of high school when he and two other students were caught with marijuana. According to Ed's own team code of conduct, Mark could have been kicked off the team. But Ed kept him on the squad. He told one of his assistants, "Being around the guys on the team will be good for him. He needs that positive influence."

Three years later, Mark found himself in trouble once again. Aaron and Todd both asked Ed, "Dad, why do you keep putting up with him?" His answer to both was the same: "Mark needs this team more than the team needs him." Even after Mark graduated, Ed refused to give up on him. Whenever Ed ran into Mark in town or on one of Mark's occasional trips back to church, Ed went over to him, put his arm around him, and said, "You've got a good future in front of you, Mark. I know it."

Mark never came out to the football field to help with the cleanup, but his father certainly did.

Within the first couple of days Ed asked Dave and some of the other football dads to supervise the students as they cleared the field, tore down the chain-link fence, dismantled bleachers, and tended to anything else that had to be done. Once the field was back under construction, Ed asked Dave and the dads to take a crew and start clearing the space where the team's makeshift locker room would be. That building would become the school bus barn once the school was rebuilt. In the meantime, the Falcons had to have a place in which to change clothes and take showers if they were going to play any home games. Dave jumped on it.

On this day, contractors, not volunteers, were Ed's primary concern. He sat at his desk and looked over his schedule. Bricklayers were supposed to arrive soon to build the low walls around the back of the baseball and softball fields. Most high schools ran chain-link fence all the way to the ground for their backstops, but Ed wanted something better. He saw the rebuilding of the athletic facilities as his chance to provide the best settings of any high school in Iowa, maybe even the country. Brick below the backstops gave the A-P fields the same look as major league parks, like Wrigley Field. The school's insurance didn't cover such extras, which is why Ed worked so hard to raise extra money for the athletic department after the storm.

It wasn't just that Ed wanted all the sports to have the best. Every small school district in Iowa lived in fear of being consolidated into another district. Aplington and Parkersburg lived through this once, when A-P High School was formed. By building state-of-the-art facilities for everything from a field for the girls' softball team to a space for the wrestling team to the gym where the volleyball and basketball teams played, as well as a first-rate football field, Ed was making it harder for the state legislators to shut down A-P and move them off to Grundy Center or Dike-New Hartford. However, his passion for the best increased his workload considerably.

✦ ✦ ✦

While Ed toiled away at his makeshift office on the hill overlooking the football field, Jan opened city hall for business — or at least the building the town used as city hall. The tornado swept away the actual city hall, and with it all the records that allowed the town to conduct business. On her first day back at work, Jan didn't have so much as pencil and paper to work with. She had pencil and paper now, along with a computer, but she was still waiting for the town's lost computer data to be recovered.

A line of people were waiting for Jan when she arrived at the temporary city hall, just as they did every morning. She took her place behind the counter and motioned for the first person in line to come over. As with everyone else in town, Jan had known this woman for years. "What can I do for you today, Mrs. Smith?"

"Hi, Jan, honey. I have a little problem with my water bill. I paid my bill last month, but when I got my bank statement, my check didn't show up. I called the bank, and they said the check never came through. Now, I know I paid it, and I sure don't want my water to be shut off."

"When did you make your last payment?" Jan asked.

"Right at the end of May. I remember because I dropped it off in the night deposit box on Saturday morning."

"Did that happen to be the Saturday before Memorial Day?"

Mrs. Smith's eyes lit up. "Why, yes, it did. How did you know?"

"Your check was blown away with city hall that weekend. Don't worry. You won't have to pay a late charge. I'll make a note that your last payment was lost in the tornado." Jan recited those lines at least ten times a day, and every time she was amazed that people did not make the connection between the storm and their lost checks.

The next person in line had another familiar problem. "Hey, Jan," a man said, "I, uh, I got a sewer bill today, but I don't have a house. How can I be billed for a house that doesn't exist anymore?"

"The billing cycle starts on the fifteenth of the month. The bill is for the second half of May when you still had a house," Jan explained.

"Still, doesn't it seem odd to you that I got a bill for using the sewer in a house that's not there anymore?"

"The bill is prorated so that it only covers the part of the month when your house was still there. We had to estimate the bills the best we could, but it is only half of what it would have been if your house were still there."

The man started to argue the point further but stopped short. Everyone in town knew Ed and Jan were in the same boat as the other two hundred homeowners who had lost their homes.

During her lunch hour, Jan ran over to her house to check on the builders. The walls were up, which made her smile. She could see the walls three blocks away, since nothing stood to block her view as she drove up. Getting out, she walked around her lot. She nearly tripped over a piece of wood protruding out of the ground. "I don't think we will ever get everything cleaned up in the yard," she said.

By 1:00 p.m., she was back at her desk. By 6:00, the flow of people had slowed down enough to allow the office to close for the day. She went back to the worksite and then headed off to Cedar Falls for her daily shopping trip. Sometime around 8:00 in the evening, she arrived back at the apartment over True Value Hardware.

Ed had only been home a few minutes when Jan arrived. Before either could say much to the other, his cell phone rang. "Yeah. OK. Now? I guess now will work. I'll be there in a couple of minutes." He hung up his phone and said, "I'm sorry, but I have to go. There's a reporter from the *New York Times* over at the school, wanting to ask me a few questions. I'll be back as soon as I can."

"That's fine," Jan said. "I'll be here."

With that, Ed was out the door. After the interview was over, he went down to the football field and checked on the watering system. A turf expert told Ed that keeping water on the field was the key to coaxing grass back into the gashes left by the debris on the field. That was easier said than done. When the tornado drove boards, sheet metal, lawn mower decks, and even a trailer axle into the football field, it drove them so deep into the turf that the underground irrigation pipes snapped in two. Ron Westerman, head custodian at the middle school, who worked side by side with Ed in restoring the field, spent what felt like an eternity chasing down leaks in the pipes. Even once he had repaired every break, he periodically had to shut down the entire system to flush out rocks and dirt left behind by damage to the system.

Ed dropped by that evening to check on what was coming out of every sprinkler head and to make sure that the generator running the whole system was still up and running. He felt like he had turned back the clock to the days when he had to manually move the irrigation pipes from one end of the field to the other.

Sometime around 10:00, Ed climbed back up the stairs to his apartment. Jan was already asleep. Ed sat down in the living room and turned on the television to check the score of the Yankee-Red Sox game. Ed loved the Yankees; he had his entire life. After less than a half inning he fell asleep in front of the TV. Sometime during the top half of the ninth inning he woke up and went to bed.

Long before the first light peeked through the windows of the small apartment over True Value Hardware, the alarm went off. Ed stumbled over to his dresser, dug out his clothes for the day, and headed for the shower. Today would be a rerun of the day before, as would the next day, and the next and the next. This would prove to be a very long, yet very fast, summer.

CHAPTER 9

HALFTIME

Good things happen to good people.
ED THOMAS

ED LOOKED AT HIS WATCH AND THEN CROSSED HIS ARMS AND tapped his foot. "Leave it to Todd to be late for his own wedding."

"Oh, Ed," Jan said. "He's not late for his wedding. This is only the rehearsal. It's not a big deal."

Ed looked at his watch again. "You know how I can't stand starting late. When I do something, we start on time, and we end on time. But how can we start on time without a groom?"

"It's OK, Ed. Relax," Jan said.

Ed looked up at her and paused for a moment. Relaxing had become a foreign concept to both of them in the eight weeks since the tornado. He gave Jan his little half-smile smirk. "I don't know if I remember how."

That struck Jan as funny. "Well, then, it's about time you get back in practice. This weekend is going to be wonderful. Let's enjoy it."

Ed knew Jan was right. This was going to be his first and only break of the summer, and he needed to enjoy it. With only seven weeks left to get the field ready for the first home game, there was only one thing that could get him to walk away from work for the next few days. Actually, there were two, but both focused on his sons. One was Todd's wedding; the other was a trip to New York

City with Aaron. Ed had always talked about going to a game at Yankee Stadium. So when a reporter from New York told Ed she could get him a couple of tickets, Jan talked him into going with Aaron. She said the trip would be a birthday present from her, so there was no reason for him not to go. The Yankees were building a brand-new ballpark next door to "The House That Ruth Built," which meant that this summer was their last opportunity to go to a game there.

"You're right," Ed said. "It is going to be a great weekend. And if Todd would ever get here, we could get started."

Jan rolled her eyes and shook her head. "Oh, Ed." In truth, she needed a reminder on how to relax as much as her husband did. Back in May, she couldn't think about anything else besides the wedding. She had three dresses hanging in her closet that she had ordered online as possibilities to wear for the wedding. Ellie and Candice were supposed to help her choose which one to keep, and she planned on returning the other two. Unfortunately, the tornado carried away all three, which meant Jan had to go buy a fourth dress in between shopping for plumbing fixtures for their house.

Besides shopping for her dress, she had not had time to help Candice with anything wedding related. But now that the big day had finally arrived, Jan made up her mind to think about nothing else except enjoying the Todd and Candice celebration. The town, the house, the football field—all of it could take care of itself for a few days. This mid-July weekend was a time for family, and nothing but family. Jan and Ed both desperately needed it.

Around 5:45 p.m., Todd and the groomsmen walked into the foyer of the church. "Hey, look who decided to show up for his own wedding rehearsal," Ed said. "Glad you could join us, Todd."

"Sorry we're late. It took a little longer to get eighteen holes in than we thought."

"Hmm, your buddies must have been letting you win to keep you out there that long," Ed said.

"Ha. *Let me win* nothing. I was on fire out there. Too bad you weren't there, old man, or I would have shown you a thing or two about golf."

Ed broke out into a huge grin. "You just keep telling yourself that, pal. You just keep telling yourself that."

"Yeah, right," Todd said. "So did I miss anything?"

"We went ahead and had the whole thing without you. Found Candice a groom who can tell time," Ed said.

"That's a good one, Dad." Todd and Ed always bantered back and forth whenever they got together, especially on the golf course. Just because Todd was getting married, Ed didn't see any reason to hold back on this day.

"Thanks. By the way," Ed said, "did you talk to Candice about postponing the honeymoon so that you can come to New York with me and Aaron?"

"Have you lost your mind, Dad?"

"Oh, come on, she'll understand."

"I think you've been working out in the sun too long." Ed and Todd were still ribbing each other when Candice walked in from the church auditorium. "Are we ready?" she said.

Ed and Todd looked at one another. "Sure," Todd said. "Sorry I'm late, babe."

"No big deal," Candice said. "We needed to work on the music anyway."

Todd took Candice by the hand and walked off toward the rest of the waiting wedding party. Ed went over and put his arm around Jan. "Todd hit the jackpot when he found her," Jan said.

"You better believe it," Ed said. Ed knew Candice was someone special not long after she and Todd started dating. At the time, Todd was Ed's quarterbacks coach, a position he had held for five years, going back to his junior year at Wartburg College. However, once he started dating Candice, Todd came to his father and said, "Dad, I need to step away from coaching for a while." When Ed asked why, Todd said, "You know, I have a new job, and I really need to get established there. And I met this girl . . ." He didn't have to say anything more. Ed told Todd that he understood. Later, Ed confided to a friend that he had never been prouder of Todd than in that moment. "It took quite a man to stand up to his father like that," Ed said.

◆ ◆ ◆

The day of the wedding started off hot and sticky, a classic Iowa July day. The air conditioner in the front room of Ed and Jan's shotgun apartment had little effect in the back, where their bedroom was. "I'm glad we're going to get away from here, if only for one night," Jan said.

Ed walked out of the bathroom. "Yeah." He paused and a look came over his face that Jan recognized.

"What's wrong?" she asked.

"I'm having second thoughts about going to New York. I have so much work that has to get done."

"It will be here when you get back. Go. You and Aaron will have a great time."

"I suppose you're right," Ed said with a tone that made it clear he was far from convinced.

Ed and Jan arrived at the church two hours before the start of the wedding. Unlike the night before, Todd was already there, along with Candice, her parents, and the rest of the wedding party. The photographer had already started lining people up for pictures. "Glad you finally decided to show up," Todd said to his father.

Ed quickly looked at his watch. "Whaddya talkin' about? We're early."

"Is that what you call it?"

Ed shook his head. "Hey," he said changing the subject, "did you talk Candice into postponing the honeymoon so you could go to New York with me and Aaron?"

Candice rolled her eyes.

"Yeah, Dad, that's going to happen. Do you think I'm nuts, or what?"

"Just thought I'd check one last time," Ed said.

He and Jan sat down on one of the pews and waited to be called up front by the photographer. A few minutes after they arrived, Aaron and Ellie and their three sons came in. The two oldest boys, Owen and Gavin, had on tuxedoes, although neither appeared to enjoy being dressed up. As soon as the boys saw Ed and Jan, they raced over and jumped up on them. Ed beamed. "Where's the birthday boy?" he asked.

"Right here," Ellie said, trying to hold on to a squirming one-year-old boy.

"This is quite a fuss for your birthday, isn't it, pal," Ed said to Trevan as the boy leaned over and held out his arms toward his grandfather. Later, at the reception, Todd and Candice would bring out a birthday cake for Trevan and lead the guests in singing "Happy Birthday" to him.

In the midst of all the prewedding photo taking and last-minute preparations, Ed walked over to Todd and put his arm around his shoulder. "I just want to tell you how proud I am of you, Todd. I really am."

"Thanks, Dad," Todd said. He saw tears streaming down Ed's face, which made Todd tear up as well. "Now don't you lose it on me, Dad, or I'll never hold it together." They both laughed.

"I'll do my best," Ed said as he slapped Todd on the back.

The two of them managed to hold it together throughout the service, although Todd nearly lost it when his father hugged him and told him he loved him after Todd escorted Jan in. Later Ed read 1 John 4:7–12 as part of the ceremony. After he finished, he and Jan sat on the front pew, one grandson between them and another next to Jan. They teared up when Todd and Candice exchanged vows and applauded when the pastor pronounced them husband and wife. Jan was thrilled to have another girl in the family, although Ed informed Candice at the reception, "We expect grandsons." He was only half kidding.

Todd and Candice arranged to hold the reception in a ballroom connected to a hotel in Waterloo. The two of them asked Ed to give the opening prayer. Before he prayed, Ed looked over at Todd and Candice and said, "I don't have a lot of fatherly advice to give except for this. Always, always put God first in your relationship. And after that, make sure you put one another and your family ahead of anyone, or anyone else besides God." All his life, Todd had heard his father say the same thing. However, on this day, sitting with his new bride in front of all their friends and family, his dad's words struck him like they never had before.

◆ ◆ ◆

Sometime around 9:30 the next evening, Ed's phone rang. "Dad, we have a problem," Aaron said. "The airline just called. Our flight out of Cedar Rapids has been canceled. They had some kind of problem with the plane. However, they can get us on a flight out of Moline, but it leaves really early."

"How early?" Ed asked.

"You're probably going to have to leave Parkersburg around 1:30 for us to get there on time."

"1:30 a.m.?"

"Yep."

"Not a problem. I'll let the other guys know, and we'll pick you up around 2:15."

True to his word, Ed and a friend pulled into Aaron's driveway in La Porte City right on time. Thunderstorms rolled through the area when they arrived at Quad City International Airport in Moline, Illinois, two and a half hours later. A small tornado hit the area right after their flight took off. Theirs was one of the last flights out before the airport shut down because of the weather. After a layover in Chicago, they arrived at La Guardia Airport in New York early in the afternoon.

Ed and Aaron and the two friends who made the trip with them took a cab to their midtown Manhattan hotel. Watching the city pass outside the window, Ed said, "Wow, I don't know why people want to live like this."

"What do you mean, Dad?"

"All crammed together with all this traffic. It's not me."

"So I guess that means we don't have to worry about you moving here anytime soon, then?" Aaron said.

"Uh, no."

They checked into the hotel and had just enough time to grab something to eat before it was time to go to the ballpark. Ed wanted to get there early enough to see the monuments in the outfield at Yankee Stadium and to just take in "The House That Ruth Built." Instead of paying for a cab to make the long drive to the Bronx, they walked over to Grand Central Station and took the subway. Crowds pressed into the subway car. Ed looked over at Aaron and mouthed, "I hate this."

Aaron just shook his head and smiled. Once Ed was able to work his way closer to Aaron, he said, "If I had to do this to get to work every day, I wouldn't work, or maybe I would live in my office."

"It's not that bad," Aaron said. "I wouldn't want to do this every day, but it's not a big deal for this one time. At least now you can say you've experienced a New York subway."

"I guess," Ed said.

Aaron sensed that something more than the crowded subway car was bothering his father. "What's wrong, Dad?"

"I'm feeling a little guilty about taking off like this."

"Why?"

"There's just so much work to be done, and we don't have much time to finish it."

"You know, Dad, the work will still be there when you get back. How many years have you been talking about going to a game at Yankee Stadium? When are we ever going to get a chance to do something like this again?"

"You're right. But still ..."

"Don't worry about it. Let's have fun."

"All right."

When the four of them walked up the ramp at Yankee Stadium, Ed stopped thinking about work. "I don't know that I've ever seen greener grass," Ed said. They toured the stadium, snapped pictures of everything, and then found their seats in the right–center field stands. When the first pitch was thrown, Aaron looked over at his father. "I haven't seen you like this in a long time," Aaron said.

Ed just smiled. "Thanks for making me do this," he said. "This is great. I'm glad we got to do this together."

"So am I," Aaron said.

The subway was not quite as crowded after the game. Ed sat back and studied the subway map hanging on the train wall. A couple who was wearing Yankee gear walked up to the map and started discussing where they should get off.

"I think I can help you," Ed said. "Where is it you're trying to go?"

They told him.

"OK, you need to take the 82nd Street stop. That will put you right there."

Across the aisle Aaron nearly fell over laughing. "Since when did you become such an expert on getting around New York City?"

Ed gave him his patented half-smile smirk. "What do you want me to do? Let these poor people wander around lost in the big city?"

"Maybe you ought to move here after all," Aaron said.

"Hmm, maybe I will," Ed joked. "Maybe I will."

CHAPTER 10

A SUMMER
OF CHANGE

You either get better or you get worse.
You never stay the same.
ED THOMAS

IN 1975, THE ONLY THING ED KNEW ABOUT PARKERSBURG was that it needed a football coach. He accepted a job interview, but only as a backup plan. Before the interview, he went home to What Cheer to talk to his friend Tom Teeple about the place. "I'm looking for a new job and a step up. I have two interviews next week, one in Allison and one in Parkersburg," Ed said.

That grabbed Teep's attention. Although he was not originally from Parkersburg, he and his wife, Sue, had lived there for a couple of years right after he graduated from barber college. "I love Parkersburg, but they don't have much of a program," Teep said, and then added, "and Allison has all the studs."

"Yep," Ed said with a confident smile.

"Why don't you stay at Northeast Hamilton?" Teep asked.

"Can't. I already quit. I turned in my resignation as soon as I got the job interviews at Parkersburg and Allison. I've been at Northeast three years. I figure I'll spend three years, maybe four, at the next place and just work my way up the ladder."

To Teep, it seemed clear which job Ed would take. "Allison would be a good next step."

"That's what I was thinking." Two weeks later, Teep was surprised when Ed came back to his barbershop and announced, "Well, I took the Parkersburg job."

Teep couldn't believe his ears. "What about Allison?"

"They offered it to me," Ed said, "but only after I'd already given a verbal commitment to Parkersburg. I wasn't going to go back on my word. Besides, I was impressed with the community and the school administration in Parkersburg. I think it has a lot to offer."

"As a good next step."

"I think so."

Five years into Ed's three-year plan, Parkersburg played for its first state championship. That made him decide to stick around a little longer. In all, he led Parkersburg to the state championship game twice, and Aplington-Parkersburg, after the two schools merged, four times, winning two titles. That level of success made Ed a hot commodity on the coaching front. A couple of years after Parkersburg played in the state championship game for the first time, Tom Teeple was working as an umpire at a baseball tournament in another town. The athletic director of the town's high school came up to him and said, "We're getting your football coach. I offered Ed Thomas the job as our head football coach, and he's going to take it."

"Did he sign a contract yet?" was Teep's only response.

"Well, no," the AD said.

"Uh, OK," Teep replied with a tone that said more than his words.

The next morning, Teep got together for coffee with Ed and their usual coffee crew, which included Jim Graves, the man who coined the phrase "the Sacred Acre" while giving Ed a hard time about the amount of time he spent working on his field. The moment Ed walked in, Teep said, "So you gonna need some help moving?"

"What are you talking about?" Ed said.

"I was umpiring over in Independence last night, and the AD there told me you're taking a job there. They have a pretty good program. I can see why you're interested in it, although I think we've got a pretty good program right here," Teep said.

Ed shook his head in disbelief that the word had slipped out. "We're considering it, but I haven't made up my mind yet," he said.

Later that afternoon, Ed came into Teep's barbershop and announced, "We're not going."

Several years later, Simpson College offered Ed a job as its head football coach. Aaron and Todd had finished high school by this point. As Ed considered it, Jan told him, "If you're going to make a move, this is the perfect time." The job tempted him. After all, he had always dreamed of moving up to the college ranks. Every high school coach does, just as every college coach dreams of moving up to the pros. While Simpson was a small school, it offered Ed opportunities he could never dream about in a town like Parkersburg. Ed nearly took the job, but he finally decided to stay put.

No, Ed never imagined he would stay in Parkersburg forever, but those closest to him were not surprised. They knew how much he loved the town, and they saw the impact he had on his players. Frosty Westering's book *Make the Big Time Where You Are* encouraged Ed that he was on the right track in his belief that bigger doesn't always mean better. On top of that, all of his and Jan's closest friends lived in Parkersburg.

Yet the single biggest reason Ed settled down for good in Parkersburg came down to one peculiar quirk in his personality: he hated change. Once he found something that worked, he stuck with it. In 1978, three years after he came to Parkersburg, he watched Emmetsburg High School run the "quick huddle"—that is, the offense breaks its huddle, runs to the line of scrimmage, and snaps the ball before the defense can get set. Ed liked it so much that he ran it in Parkersburg that season, and every other season for the next thirty years. He also used the same playbook year after year after year. Players who suited up for him in 2007 ran essentially the same plays he used back in 1987. Ed joked that he only had five offensive plays, which was not far from the truth. Opposing coaches knew exactly what A-P's offense would throw at them. Yet knowing what play is coming and stopping it are two different things. Ed prided himself on having his teams in such good physical condition and so prepared for game night that they would outhustle and outlast their opponents.

Yes, Ed hated change, yet that was exactly what he faced nearly every minute of every day throughout the summer following the tornado. His life, his team, his community, his family — everything was in flux. The biggest change of all came at the school.

Aplington-Parkersburg High School was Ed's mission field, his church, the place to which God had called him to make a difference in the lives of students. In July, just under two months after the tornado, a train of dump trucks and flatbed trailers carrying back hoes, excavators, and bulldozers pulled into the parking lot of Ed's mission field. Slowly but surely over the next two weeks, demolition crews finished off what the tornado had started.

Watching the school come down, piece by piece, day by day, didn't help the mood in Parkersburg. It felt like a protracted funeral. A group of students sat on the grass below the elementary school, right across the street from the high school, and wept. Periodically other students and their parents joined them. Every once in a while, someone pulled out a camera and snapped a few pictures. However, most people just sat and stared. They didn't want to take any pictures. Most preferred to remember the school the way it was before the storm.

On the last day of the demolition, Chris Luhring drove out to the golf course looking for Ed. If this had been a normal summer, the golf course would have been the first place Chris went to find him instead of the last. But this summer was anything but normal, and today was an especially abnormal day, and not just because Ed had taken a rare afternoon off.

"Hey, Coach, how ya doing?" Chris asked.

"Any day when I get to play golf is a good day," Ed said with a smile.

"Yeah. You haven't been able to do much of that this summer. So how did you do?"

"Played the front nine a few strokes over par. Didn't do too bad considering how little I've played lately."

"That's good. Yeah, well, I just wanted to check and make sure you were OK, Coach. I better get back to work."

"So what's really going on, Chris? I know you didn't drive all the way out here to ask about my golf game."

Chris smiled. "Sure I did."

"I know they finished tearing the school down today," Ed said. "It's all right. I would be lying if I said it didn't bother me. That's why I'm here instead of there. A friend told me I shouldn't be there when they tore the last of it down, and he was right. So, yeah, it's eating at me a little."

"I'm sorry, Coach. I know how much the school means to you. It means a lot to all of us."

"Thanks, Chris. I appreciate your concern. Don't worry about me, though. I'll be all right. After all, the demolition crew is just finishing what the tornado started. Besides, we've got to clear the site if we're going to get into the new building by the start of school a year from now. Me and the principal and superintendent have already started talking about what we want to put in the plans for the new school. This is our chance to give Aplington and Parkersburg a state-of-the-art facility without passing a bond issue or raising taxes or any of the other things school districts have to do to build a new building."

Chris knew his old coach meant every word, but he could tell this was a tough day for Ed. "Just like the football field, uh, Coach? Gonna build it back better than before."

Ed smiled. "Yeah, something like that," he said.

"So, you going to play the back nine?" Chris asked.

"No," Ed said, "I need to get back to work."

✦ ✦ ✦

A week or so later, Ed called the school superintendent, Jon Thompson. "Jon, you've gotta come see this!" Ed said. "The lights are up!"

"What?" Jon asked.

"The lights are up. The guys from Musco Lighting just finished installing the last of the lights. They don't have any electricity yet, but all the light poles are up on all the fields—football, baseball, softball, tennis. You can't believe how good they look."

"Hey, Coach, turn around," Jon said. "I'm parked right behind you."

Ed spun around. When he saw Jon, he broke out in a huge grin and waved. Jon walked over to him and the two of them stood and stared and took it all in. The new light poles looked nothing like the old. Before, the lights hung atop wooden poles, sort of like extra-tall telephone poles. Not the new ones. Musco Lighting installed steel poles on every one of the athletic fields. With no trees or houses or any other buildings on the south side of town to block the view, you could see the metal poles shining in the sun for miles around. Not only did Musco install the lights; they donated the lights for the football field. Originally, they had offered to install the same kind of lights that the field had before. Ed wanted to kick it up a notch and install stronger, brighter lights. When he told Musco Lighting what he wanted, the company told him, "Sure. No problem. Whatever you need."

Ed and Jon didn't say a word for a few minutes as they stood and stared at the new light poles. Below them, workers cut I-beams for the new bleachers. From the far side of the football field they heard a cement truck backing up to pour more concrete near the visitors' stands. "It's going to happen," Ed said. "We're going to pull this off."

"You know, Coach, I think you're right," Jon said.

♦ ♦ ♦

Two weeks later, Jon's cell phone rang again. Coach was calling. Jon glanced at his watch. It was after 9:00 p.m. The sun had slipped below the horizon, although it was not yet completely dark.

"Are you still in town?" Ed asked.

"No, why?"

"Meet me at the school."

"Why? Is there a problem?"

"Jon, do I only call you when something's gone wrong? Wait, don't answer that. Anyway, no. There isn't a problem. Just meet me at the school. You'll see why."

Jon got in his car and headed toward Parkersburg. His son, Alec, was already there working out with the football team.

Long before he got close to the school, he knew why Ed wanted to see him. The entire south side of town was dark, just like it was every night. No streetlights. No house lights, nothing. That side of town had been dark for so long that the blackness looked normal.

But not tonight. There in the distance Jon saw the lights of the football field shining bright. By the time he got to the field, a crowd had already started to form. Football players and their parents walked around on the Sacred Acre like they had never seen light before. Adults laughed while players high-fived each other. The Fourth of July had already passed, but to Jon and the people dancing across the field, it felt like the Fourth of July and Christmas rolled into one.

The superintendent found Ed and gave him a hug. "Have you ever seen anything so beautiful in all your life?" Ed said to him.

Jon grinned. "No, I can't say that I have."

Ed left the lights on for nearly an hour. No one wanted to leave the party. The A-P Falcons would not play their first game for nearly a month, and the bleachers, scoreboard, fencing, press box, and everything else needed for the game were far from finished. But on this night that didn't seem to matter. The first light on the south side of town came from the Sacred Acre, from the field where Ed's team played football, like a city shining on a hill. For the town of Parkersburg, it now felt like they had turned a corner. The town was not the same as it was on May 24, and it never would be again. But in the light of this night, the future never looked brighter.

CHAPTER 11

FIRST GLIMPSE
OF NORMALCY

*If we do what's right, get better every day,
winning will take care of itself.*
ED THOMAS

IN 1995, APLINGTON-PARKERSBURG ENTERED THE SEASON one year removed from their first Iowa Class 1A state championship. On paper, it looked like they had a strong chance of going all the way again. Although they had lost fullback and defensive lineman Brad Meester, who had moved on to the University of Northern Iowa and then ultimately to the NFL, sophomore Aaron Kampman looked more than ready to fill his shoes. As young and inexperienced as Aaron was, Ed could tell he had the tools to be something special.

A-P opened the season at home against East Marshall on Labor Day weekend with high hopes for the season. A funny thing happened in that first game. Someone forgot to inform East Marshall that they were supposed to be intimidated by the mighty Falcons. A-P came out flat, and East Marshall seized the opportunity. No matter what Ed tried, the Falcons never got on track. East Marshall came away with a victory in a game Ed knew his Falcons would have won if they had played anywhere near their potential.

School was out for Labor Day on Monday, but Ed made his team come in for practice. The players, including his oldest son, Aaron, dragged themselves out onto the practice field, heads hanging low for what they called Black Monday. Monday practices after a loss were bad; the Labor Day practice after a loss was the worst of the worst.

Ed pulled his team over to a shady spot next to a storage shed. "Have a seat, fellas," he said before practice began. "We need to talk." The players found spots on the grass and sat in a mass circle around Ed. Assistant coaches Al Kerns, Jon Wiegmann, and Greg Fisher, each of whom had coached with Ed for years, stood in the back, arms crossed, smiles on their faces, wondering what he had up his sleeve today. While most coaches would launch into a tirade after such a disappointing loss, Ed always had something memorable planned to get the team's attention after a big loss.

"Fellas," Ed began, "I don't have to tell you that Friday night's game was not our best effort. I don't know what we were doing out there, but I know this: We didn't play like a team." He then reached over and picked up a large jar filled with beans. "It's kinda like this," he said. Popping open the jar, he dropped a rubber ball inside. "The ball cannot float on its own," he said as the ball sank to the bottom. He then screwed the lid back on and held up the jar.

"That ball and our season are a lot alike. Right now, it feels like both are sinking, but they don't have to be." He then began to swirl the jar around and around. As he did, the beans lifted the ball up toward the top of the jar. "You see, fellas, Friday night, we went out on that field and played like a bunch of individuals. Well, I gotta tell you, if we do that, our season will sink like this ball. But when we work together like these beans are, we can lift up this season and win games and reach the goals we set back in the spring." Players' heads started nodding in agreement.

Suddenly, Ed whirled around and slammed the jar against the wall of the shed behind him. The jar of beans exploded. "And that's what's going to happen to your season if we don't start coming together as a team!" Ed shouted. "But Friday we're busting out. Now who's ready to get to work?"

The entire team jumped up and shouted.

Al Kerns slapped Jon Wiegmann on the back. "He's always got something," he said. "Ed always finds a way to get through to 'em."

They won their next game 40 to 6.

✦ ✦ ✦

Ed had the same high hopes for his 2008 team, or at least he did prior to May 25. The previous season, the team won its first eight games by an average score of 35 to 5. The offense scored more than forty points four times, and the defense didn't give up a single point until the third game of the season. However, they lost a nail-biter on the road to Starmont High School in the last game of the regular season, 28 to 25. Five days later, they played their worst game of the year against Newman Catholic in the first game of the state playoffs. The Falcons' 2007 season ended with a disappointing 38 to 13 defeat. Even so, Ed could not wait for the next year. With a strong core of returning seniors, he thought this team could be special. Throw in some talented juniors, and it might just have what it takes to go all the way. For Ed, football season could not come fast enough.

Yet in the wake of the tornado, Ed's team had already suffered a devastating loss before a single down had been played. Although only ten of his players' families lost their homes, everyone on the team was affected by the storm in one way or another. Every single player had either a grandparent, aunt or uncle, or close friend whose home had been destroyed. Those who had lost their homes were now scattered across different communities in the area while they rebuilt their houses in Parkersburg. Ed wasn't sure if those living temporarily in places like New Hartford and Grundy Center would be eligible to stay enrolled at A-P, much less play football. The team had the talent to go far, but Ed had coached talented teams in the past that didn't fare well. Winning teams needed more.

And then there was the problem of focus. Since the day he took his first head coaching position in 1972, Ed demanded his players' undivided attention as soon as football practice began. In his first year at Parkersburg, he ruffled a lot of feathers when he laid down the law to the farm kids on his team. One of his starters skipped school to help his dad pick corn. Ed cornered him the next day and told him, "You have to make a choice. You're either going to play football or you're going to help your dad farm. You can't do both." With the rebuilding in town under way, Ed wondered how he could capture his players' attention in the same way. It's hard to focus on a game when something much bigger surrounds you.

When the first few players ran out onto the practice field, Ed's doubts about getting his team up for the season evaporated. His seniors showed up early and sprinted out like ten-year-olds fleeing the school building on the last day of school. "Hey, Alec," Ed called out to his senior quarterback, Alec Thompson, "you ready to play a little football?"

"Are you kidding me, Coach? After all the work we did this summer, today feels like the start of summer vacation!"

"Attaboy," Ed said with a smile. He walked away and said to himself, "I have a feeling this season is going to be special."

The rest of the team showed up with the same kind of enthusiasm. It wasn't just the start of practice that had them fired up. The tornado had made national news, and the story did not end when other natural disasters grabbed the headlines. News crews from local television stations were out in full force that first practice, and the players noticed. When the lights of the cameras came on, the players jumped around and screamed and chanted with just a little more enthusiasm than normal.

"OK, fellas, gather in over here," Ed called out to formally start practice. The team huddled around him. "Go ahead and take a knee," he said. "Now, guys, I don't have to tell you that this off-season has been different from any other year. But you know, even with everything going on and with all the work you fellas put into helping here at the school and around town, we had a really good summer in the weight room and in our conditioning program. And we had a good three-day camp for all the linemen last week.

"Now today we're going to get down to actually getting ready for this season. I don't know about you fellas, but it feels really good to me to be back out here on this field again and to just think about football for a change. This has been quite a summer. You've faced more adversity in the past three months than most people face in their lifetimes, and you didn't let it beat you down, you didn't let it define you or defeat you. Instead you made a choice to come together as a team and to work hard to clean up our field and to help people in town put their lives back together. Nothing we face this season will come close to what you've already overcome. I don't know what's going to happen this season, but I can tell you this: We're already champions!

"Now get on your feet!" The team leaped into the air. "Where're you from?" Ed yelled.

"A-P!" the team called back.

"Where're you from?" Ed yelled louder.

"A-P!" the team shouted.

"Where're you from?" Ed yelled.

"A-P!" the team screamed so loud it nearly knocked Ed over.

"So let's get out there and get after it! Linemen over there. Defensive backs over there. Quarterbacks and receivers, over there!" With that, the team sprinted out across the practice field like they were running out for the start of the Super Bowl. Ed wasn't quite sure, but he could have sworn that two or three players' feet didn't even touch the ground. It was going to be quite a season.

Emotions weren't so high the next morning. Humidity levels were off the charts, and the August heat cranked up the moment the sun poked up over the horizon. The seniors on the team tried to keep everyone on track, but about three-quarters of the way through practice, most of the underclassmen were moving at half speed, if that fast. Ed had seen enough.

"Gather in here guys!" he yelled. "Now! Run! We don't walk on this field! Get in here!" As soon as the last player joined the group, Ed dropped the hammer. "You fellas think you're hurting? You think you've got it bad? Well, look around! You see all those houses that are gone? You haven't suffered. Those are the people who are suffering! We're playing for them. So quit dragging and GET UP AND GET GOING! YOU SEE ALL THOSE PEOPLE REBUILD- ING! IT'S NO DIFFERENT HERE!"

For the players in that circle, the jar of beans hit the wall. It was time to get to work.*

---

*For footage of the early season A-P football practices, go to *www.youtube.com/ watch?v=kx1yBKIKSLs&feature=channel*.

CHAPTER 12

MORE THAN A GAME

It's all right here now.
You've just got to go take it.
ED THOMAS

FOOTBALL SEASON ALWAYS KEPT ED KEYED UP, BUT NOT LIKE this. In just over twelve hours, his team would run onto its home field to play West Marshall, exactly 105 days after it had looked like an impossibility. He bounced out of bed as giddy as an eight-year-old boy on Christmas morning.

After a quick shower, he got dressed and ran down the apartment stairs. Not even the raindrop that bounced on top of his head the moment he walked outside could dampen his mood. He looked up at the sky and broke out in a smile. *Ah, who cares if it rains or not? We're playing football tonight, and we're doing it here.*

Ed hopped into his truck and took off toward the football field. Ron Westerman, who had worked side by side with Ed on the field all summer, was already hard at work when Ed arrived. "Hey, Ron," Ed said as he bounced out of his truck, "tonight's the night!"

Ron shook his head and let out a nervous laugh. "Lotta work to be done between now and then, Coach, a lotta work. I'm not sure if we can finish it all."

Ed walked over and patted Ron on the back. "Don't worry. It will all come together. We've come too far not to."

Ron looked around at his fellow school employees scrambling around the field that morning. The head of the maintenance staff at the high school was laying sod around the FieldTurf coaches' box on the visitors' side of the field. One of Ed's former students, who was now an electrician, was on a ladder under the scoreboard, hooking something up to the electronic message board. A couple of other guys from the school maintenance staff were hammering forms into the ground next to the ticket booths, where concrete was to be poured later that morning. Still another had started stringing extension cords over to the concession stands. "Yeah, I know, Coach. We'll get everything done. I don't know how, but we'll get it done."

"You bet we will. I've got to get to class. I'll be back this afternoon. Call me if you need me."

As much as he hated to leave, Ed could not stay at the field for long; he had a full day of teaching ahead. He had to drive to Aplington Middle School, which now doubled as the high school. The school district had brought in portable classrooms to help make space. During two-a-days, Ed canceled the second practice of the day on more than one occasion so that his players could help move desks and set up classrooms. The middle school building felt cramped, but no one complained. After all, everyone knew this was a temporary arrangement, and it sure beat having their school district absorbed by one in a nearby town.

Once the morning bell rang, Ed tried to keep his mind on his classes, but he was clearly distracted. He wasn't alone. The school had the feel of the day before Christmas break. Even when Ed managed to focus his full attention on his lecture on the Monroe Doctrine, his cell phone would ring. "Hey, Coach, sorry to disturb you, but I have a quick question for you ..." With so many contractors, school employees, and volunteers trying to put the finishing touches on the field for the game, Ed had no choice but to take the calls. The few times he let the calls go to voice mail, he had to ask one of his students to help him retrieve the messages. In the three months since the school superintendent got him a cell phone, Ed had still not figured out how to do anything more than make and receive phone calls.

The moment classes let out, Ed rushed back to Parkersburg and the football field. He parked near the television trucks from Waterloo and Des Moines that had set up shop in the parking lot. KWWL planned on broadcasting the game live, a first for Parkersburg. It was over three hours before kickoff, yet the high school lot had already started to fill with fans gathering for the game. Ed wasn't surprised. The week before in the season opener at Dike-New Hartford, the visitors' stands were already packed when the Falcons got off the bus. Clearly, the community was as anxious for this season as Ed was. Milling about in the crowd were former players who had come back to town just for this night. Ed tried to stop and say hello to each one, but he didn't have much time for socializing.

"OK, Ron, where are we with everything?" Ed asked as soon as he found Ron Westerman.

"Well, the scoreboard is up and running. And since it finally stopped raining, we were able to get the concrete truck in here. They just finished pouring the last of it. Don't worry. They used quick-drying cement, so it should be good to go long before game time. My guys strung power cords to the concession stands and ticket booths, so that's taken care of. We did the same with water hoses for the concession stands. It may not be pretty, but they have water. And we set up the extra chairs around the track for all the special guests who are supposed to be here tonight." Ron let out a long sigh. "Soooo, all in all I would say we're ready to play a little football."

"The field is ready?"

"Oh, yeah," Ron said with a smile. "Just wait until you see it."

"Let's go," Ed said.

◆ ◆ ◆

Players and assistant coaches arrived earlier than usual. The atmosphere at Ed Thomas Field felt like a carnival had just pulled into town. Part of the carnival surrounded the arrival of Green Bay Packers defensive lineman Aaron Kampman and his wife, Linde. Even though the NFL season opened that weekend, Aaron was able to come back for the game because the Packers opened at home on Monday night. Aaron and Linde had been back several times since Aaron came into town the day after the tornado. Every time they returned, the town looked different.

As they drove through town on their way to the football field for the first game, they saw houses springing up all across the south side of town. The Kwik Star gas station was open for business, and the bank and city hall buildings were almost finished. Yet they noticed the biggest change in the town when they walked into the crowd at the Booster Club dinner. This did not feel like a town struggling to recover from a tornado. "Man, you can just feel the hope in the air," Aaron said to Linde. "You can sense a spirit of redemption here."

As soon as he could get away from family, Aaron walked over to the bus barn that doubled as the teams' temporary locker rooms. He slipped into the door, almost unnoticed. Camera crews filled the room, and microphones popped up like dandelions in spring. Ed caught sight of him and waved him over. "Man, I'm so glad you could make it back," Coach said.

"I had to see it with my own eyes," Aaron said. "Wow, I can't believe you guys pulled this off so fast."

"A lot of people put in a lot of time to make it happen. So, you ready to talk to the team?"

Aaron took a deep breath. "Are you sure you want me to talk to them? I mean, this is your night, not mine." A couple of days earlier, Aaron had called and asked Ed if he minded if he came back for the game. Ed not only told him to come; he asked Aaron to speak to the team prior to their warm-ups.

"It's not my night either. It's their night. It's the town's night. I can't think of anyone I would rather have speak to them right now than you," Ed said. He then turned to the team and said, "Hey, fellas, gather round here. I've asked one of our former players to say a few words to you guys tonight. So listen up. Aaron, come on over."

Aaron walked over into the middle of the team, all of whom were sitting at their lockers or on the floor. Looking into the faces of these fifteen-, sixteen-, and seventeen-year-old boys, he threw the speech he had planned out the window. Aaron sensed these young men carried the pressure of the community's expectations on their shoulders, as though they all felt they had to win the game or they would let down the entire town. He wanted to defuse that pressure.

"Hey, guys. It's good to be back tonight. Wow. I can't believe all the cameras and microphones in this locker room. You've got more media in here covering your game than we had in Green Bay back in January for the NFC Championship game. But you know, guys, none of this media coverage really matters. What matters tonight is for you to go out there and have fun. I've played a lot of big football games in college and the pros, but I have to tell you, there's nothing in the world that compares to putting on that Falcon uniform and going out on a Friday night to play for Coach Thomas. Nothing.

"I want to leave you with one thought as you go out there. Colossians 3:23 says, 'Whatever you do, work at it with all your heart, as working for the Lord, not for men.' That verse is true for everything you will ever do in your life. As a father, I try to be the best father I can be for the sake of Christ. As a husband, I try to be the best husband I can be for the sake of Christ. And when I run out onto the football field, I play my hardest because I play for Christ, not for myself. I want to encourage you to do that as you go out there tonight. Play for him, and have fun.

"So are you guys excited?!"

The locker room erupted.

"OK, guys, let's go warm up!" Ed called out to the team.

Ed hung back for just a moment as one of his assistant coaches led the team out to the field. "Aaron, that was great. Thanks for sharing with the guys."

"You know, Coach, I didn't say anything I didn't hear you say a thousand times."

"I don't know about that. But thanks. It means a lot to me."

Aaron reached over and gave Ed a hug. "I love you, Coach."

"Love you too, Aaron. Thanks."

✦ ✦ ✦

Ed joined the team on the field. Assistant coach Jon Wiegmann walked over to him. "Wow, Coach, I thought the field looked good before. I can't believe this. It looks like a college field. Better than a college field."

Ed smiled. "Yeah, Ron and the guys did a really good job on it, didn't they?"

"Oh, man. Did they ever! And the falcon in the middle of the field and the way the word *Falcons* is painted in the end zones—it looks like the Atlanta Falcons play here."*

"You know, Wigs, I've always wanted to do that," Ed said. "I told you we were going to make it better than it was before."

The rain that fell off and on all day kicked back up about the time the Falcons came out to warm up. No one in the standing-room-only crowd seemed to mind. Nor did anyone seem to notice the extension cords running between the concession stands or the water hoses that supplied the water. The rain could not dampen the mood of the crowd, and neither could the lack of proper bathrooms or anything else that wasn't perfect that night.

"I wish I had some great words of wisdom to share with you fellas tonight, but I don't," Ed said as he started his pregame talk to his team. In his years as a coach, he had delivered scores of speeches to his teams—before games, at practices, during halftimes, after big wins and devastating losses—but nothing compared to this. Since the day he announced the team would play its first home

---

*World Class Athletic Surfaces donated both the paints and the custom-made stencils to A-P.

game on schedule, he had thought about what this moment would be like. Now that it was here, he felt that anything he said fell short of how important this moment was to himself, the team, and the entire town of Parkersburg.

"We've waited a long time for tonight. In a sense, there are two games tonight. We've already won the first one. I know a bunch of people doubted that it would be possible to get that field ready to play on this fall. We proved them wrong. There was no way we could have done this by ourselves, but we didn't have to do it by ourselves. People came in from all over this community—other students, other schools—and they made this night possible for us.

"Yes, fellas, we have already won in a lot of ways. We made a choice to get back up off the ground; we made the choice to rebuild; we made the choice to move forward! And that's something you are going to carry with you the rest of your life.

"When we run out on the field tonight, we're going to run under our old Falcon Country sign from our old scoreboard. A lot of people asked why we put it back up. It's all dented and smashed. But that sign symbolizes what our community and our town are all about. Tonight, and every night, when we go out on the field, that sign will be there to mark forever what took place here.

"I've thought a lot about tonight and what it was going to be like to go back out on our field. I hope you guys realize how truly blessed we are and the grace that has been shown to us. You guys have been a source of hope for this community. Our community is proud of you. They are proud of this program. They are proud of what it stands for.

"Tonight, every player who has ever played on that field, I guarantee you, is thinking about you. Every single one of them.

"This night is for you guys. Enjoy it. Play with heart. Play with great enthusiasm. Play the kind of football we play here at A-P for four full quarters. Fellas, I've been at this for thirty-six years, and let me tell you up front: Nothing is going to be greater than going out on that field on this night. Let's take a knee."

Ed then led the team in prayer. He didn't pray for a victory. He never did that. Instead he asked the Lord to protect both teams from injury and for the grace for his own team to go out and play with class and integrity. Even on a night like this, to Ed, the most important thing was not whether he won or lost, but in how he and his players represented their school, their community, and all the players who had come before them.

The moment he said Amen to end his prayer, his players erupted in cheers. "Are you ready? Let's go!" Ed said as he led his team out the door. He bounced around like this really was Christmas morning. If he hadn't been fifty-eight-years old, he may well have put on a helmet and shoulder pads himself and run out onto the field.

A-P won the coin toss and elected to receive. They took the opening kick and drove down the field. The fourth play of the game set the tone for the night. Facing a fourth and one at his own forty-three yard line, Ed went for the first down rather than sending in the punt team. His gamble proved to be no gamble at all, as the defense jumped offside when Alec Thompson changed the snap count. Seven plays later, Colin Tenney ran the ball into the end zone for the first score of the night. Stanley Tuve added the extra point, and A-P took a 7 to 0 lead.

West Marshall answered with a long touchdown drive of their own. However, their kicker pulled the extra point to the left. A-P held a one point lead at the end of the first quarter. In classic Ed Thomas fashion, the Falcons rushed for 105 yards in the quarter and passed for 0. They went on to score another touchdown on their second possession of the game. Their two-point conversion attempt failed. The Falcon defense forced a West Marshall punt on the Trojans second possession. However, a penalty penned A-P back inside its own ten yard line. Eight plays and ninety-three yards later, the Falcons extended their lead to 21 to 6, thanks in large part to a fifty yard Alex Hornbuckle run. Alec Thompson completed his first pass for the two-point conversion. However, West Marshall answered with a touchdown of its own at the end of the first half, although the two-point conversion attempt failed. A-P went into the locker room with a 21 to 12 lead.

Ed's halftime speech was simple and to the point. He put the focus on this game in light of the season that lay ahead of them. "We are one half of a football game away from one of our goals for this year," he said, "and that's to be 2 and 0 going into district play. It is all right here, right here, for us. All we have to do is take hold of it. So let's do it!"

A-P opened the second half with a strong defensive stand, followed by a ninety-eight-yard touchdown drive. Ed's defense intercepted a pass on West Marshall's next possession, which led to a long Alex Hornbuckle touchdown run. A-P never looked back. When the clock wound down, the final score was A-P 53 and West Marshall 20. Three of A-P's running backs finished with over one hundred yards rushing. Hornbuckle had over two hundred yards.*

For Ed, the best part, beyond the win, was the fact that for two hours, he and the entire community were able to think about nothing but football without feeling guilty about it.

As soon as the final gun sounded, Ed gathered his team around him and addressed the crowd. "This has been a very special night for our young people and for our community. There hasn't been a day since May 25 that I haven't thanked God for his grace and his mercy upon this community and upon our young people. If it wasn't for you as parents and as students and for you as a community and for outside people coming in and making this possible, we wouldn't be here tonight. And there is no question in my mind that we will be a better school and a better community than we ever were before. Thank you!"

Fireworks then exploded overhead. The message on the scoreboard simply read: Parkersburg is back.

Jan found Ed in the middle of the field. His emotions came flooding out. He hugged her and said, "That was special," his voice cracking.

* View highlights of the first game at *www.youtube.com/watch?v=hw0gxtNzV6w.*

"I know," Jan said, as calm as can be. "It was a big night."

Ed hugged her tight, tears streaming down his face. She gave him a quick kiss on the cheek. "Well done."

After the game, the coaches and their wives got together for their traditional postgame celebration. As soon as the party ended, Ed got in his little red truck and drove back to the converted bus barn. He had uniforms to wash, something he did after every game. Walking into the locker room, a huge smile broke out across his face. He pulled the first set of football pants up out of the large, plastic trash can where they had been soaking since the game ended. Using a bar of Lava soap, he scrubbed the grass stains on the knees. For Ed, this was how a Friday night was supposed to end.

CHAPTER 13

THE FINAL SEASON

Give me players with great effort,
and I will take them any day over talent.
Put the two together,
and you have something special.
ED THOMAS

WHEN ED ARRIVED AT THE FIELD EARLY THE NEXT MORN-
ing, Ron Westerman was waiting for him. "Divot mix ready?" Ed
asked.

"Got it right here," Ron replied, lifting up a five-gallon bucket.

"All right, let's get started." Ed and Ron did this after every
home game. The two of them walked around the field and poured
the combination of pregerminated grass seed, sand, a drying agent,
and green dye into the divots left from players' cleats the night
before. They started at the five yard line on the west end of the
field. "Hey, we've got lots of hookies down here." "Hookies" was
Ed's name for the cleat marks left by defensive linemen who dug
in as they tried to stop the Falcon offense. The divots turned, or
hooked, at the place where the A-P offensive line shoved them back
so far that the defense could no longer hold its position. Ed special-
ized in teaching offensive line play. The better his team played, the
more hookies on the field—and today this end of the field was
covered with them.

"Your guys spent a lot of time close to the end zones last night," Ron said. "I think you scored every time you touched the ball."

"The fellas played really well. I was sure proud of them," Ed replied.

Ed and Ron worked their way across the rest of the field. "Right here is where Wiegmann* got that big quarterback sack in the fourth quarter," Ed said pointing to a hole in the turf on the fifteen yard line. "And here's where Hornbuckle broke free for that seventy-yard run," he said on the thirty yard line.

"That kid went nuts last night," Ron said. "What did he have, a hundred and fifty yards?"

"Two hundred," Ed said with pride.

The night before had been an emotional Super Bowl for Ed, his team, and the entire community. But on this Saturday morning, walking around the field, fixing divots like Ed did after every home football game, the game was just a game.

And that is exactly what he needed it to be.

For more than one hundred days, every moment of nearly every day had been consumed by the aftermath of the tornado. But now Ed could relax a little. The first game had been played, and their house was almost completely rebuilt. He still had tons of work left with planning the new school, but when he walked out on the football field, none of that mattered. All that mattered was working with some eighty young men to win one game at a time, and along the way to impart lessons that he prayed would stick with them the rest of their lives.

With so much energy focused on playing the first home game, it would have been understandable if the team came out flat the next Friday night on the road against Grundy Center. The Falcons weren't even flat for their next practice, much less their next game. Every season, Ed preached to his team to practice like champions.

---

*Mike Wiegmann.

He believed that the way a team practiced was a direct indicator of how they would play on Friday night. If they gave a lackluster effort on Wednesday afternoon, that's how they would play two days later. "If we don't work hard to turn our weaknesses into strengths, I can guarantee you that every team we will play this season is working hard to exploit those weaknesses!" he said over and over. "Our goals this season have nothing to do with winning and losing. Every day we want to be better than the day before. That means we're going to practice better today than we ever have. And when the game rolls around, we're going to play like we practice. If we work hard and work together, we can do great things."

The 2008 version of the Aplington-Parkersburg Falcons took this idea and ran with it. Right from the start, it became clear to the entire coaching staff that this group of young men enjoyed being together. Because of how they had worked together clearing rubble and helping with the rebuilding, both at school and around town, they had a closer bond than any team Ed had ever coached. Two weeks after the tornado, a group of players went over to New Hartford when floodwaters swept through that town. They worked with Dike-New Hartford players to pull books and desks out of the middle school before the rising river got to it. Working together in this way developed a camaraderie that went far beyond the football field. Once they ran onto the field, the end result was a team that was far better than the sum of its parts.

In the third game of the season, A-P went on the road to Grundy Center for its first district game. "They always play us tough," Ed warned throughout the week. A-P won 60 to 13. The following week, they came back to Ed Thomas Field to go against Nashua-Plainfield. Once again, Ed warned the team that these guys were big and strong and that it would take their best effort to come out on top. A-P pulled it out, 50 to 32, in one of its closest regular season games of the year. Over its remaining five district games, A-P failed to score forty or more points only once, a 34 to 6 road win over BCLUW.* During the regular season, they averaged 48 points and five hundred yards of offense per game. A-P entered the state playoffs undefeated and ranked number one in the state. Along the way, they set an Iowa state record for rushing yardage for the season. It was, by all accounts, a very successful season.

Halfway through the season, Ed was working with the offensive line during practice. In the middle of a drill, he blew his whistle and said, "Hold on, guys. Let's hold off for a minute." Once he had everyone's attention, he said, "Fellas, I want to tell you that this season is the most fun I have ever had. I love being out here with you guys. I love coaching every year, but this year has been so much fun for me." Before any of the players could say a word in response, Ed blew his whistle and said, "All right, guards, line up."

◆ ◆ ◆

The first Saturday in October marked another victory for Ed and Jan. They moved into their newly rebuilt home. Ed didn't quite make his goal of being the first house rebuilt on the south side of town, but he was close. Only one or two houses were finished before the Thomases' house. Ed and Jan kept the same footprint their home had before the tornado. When they first started talking about what to rebuild, they agreed they did not want to sink themselves deep into debt. Their homeowners insurance paid to rebuild what they had before, and both Ed and Jan were content with that. On the inside, Jan tweaked the floor plan to make it more user-friendly. The original house was the classic hodgepodge you find with older homes in the Midwest. They had added onto it three times in their thirty-plus years there. With the new home, the entire floor plan flowed together.

Aaron and Ellie and their three sons, along with Todd and Candice, came over to help with the move-in. Like everything else that

*The high school for the communities of Beaman, Conrad, Liscomb, Union, and Whitten, Iowa.

came after the tornado, this wasn't the typical move of a couple who had been married over thirty years. Aside from their clothes, and there weren't many of those, the only thing Ed and Jan moved from their apartment to the new house was the bed Jan picked out right after they moved in over True Value Hardware. They scrapped the weathered dresser and dining room table they salvaged from the debris. All of the appliances were delivered and set up the week before they moved in. The furniture Jan bought in Cedar Falls wouldn't arrive for another few days, however, Aaron went by and picked up a couple of chairs so that Ed and Jan would at least have a place to sit in the evenings.

All through the day, people drove past the Thomases' home and honked and waved while friends stopped by to welcome them home. This was more than move-in day for the Thomases; it was a town-wide celebration that repeated itself every time a new home went up. The sense of optimism and hope that permeated the crowd during the first football game broke out all over town. Every day it seemed like someone else moved into their newly rebuilt home. By the end of the football season, the south side of town was lit up and alive. The view on Highway 57 still took some getting used to. All of the mature maple trees that had covered every block were gone. By spring, however, new trees were staked in front of almost every house. Parkersburg wasn't just back. It had sprung back to life faster and stronger than anyone, except Parkersburg itself, ever thought possible.

Ed was back in his home and in his normal routines by the time the state playoffs rolled around. Saturday mornings, he and Ron repaired divots on the field and then met with the team to find out who was dinged up from the night before. On Sundays, he and Jan went to the First Congregational Church, where Ed served as an elder and Sunday school teacher. Sunday afternoons, Ed and his coaching staff met to go over game film of their next opponent, while a television was on in the background with the live broadcast of a game featuring one of the four NFL players from Parkersburg.

Ed never got to watch the game. He had to get ready for next week's opponent.

With the start of the playoffs looming, he had little time to prepare. In Iowa, playoff games come quickly. The Falcons finished the regular season on a Friday night and played their first playoff game five days later on Wednesday. Fortunately, they opened at home, beating St. Ansgar 42 to 0. The following Monday, they faced St. Edmond High School from Fort Dodge. For the first time all season, A-P trailed with five minutes left to play in the game. However, they rallied and pulled out a 40 to 35 home victory, which placed them in the state quarterfinals. One more win meant moving on to play in the semifinals at the UNI Dome on the campus of the University of Northern Iowa in Waterloo.

However, a big obstacle stood in A-P's way. For their next game, the Falcons had to travel three hours by bus to take on the number two team in the state, the Emmetsburg E'Hawks. It was A-P's fourth game in fifteen days.

In all of Ed's years at A-P, he had never played Emmetsburg, although he had watched them play many times. Back in 1978, Ed learned his hurry-up offense from Emmetsburg's longtime coach, Duane Twait. Coach Twait had since retired, but the E'Hawks still used the hurry-up. In fact, Emmetsburg and A-P mirrored one another in terms of history, tradition, and approach to the game. However, the E'Hawks were bigger and faster than the Falcons. By this point in the season, A-P had grown accustomed to playing bigger and faster teams.

The three-hour drive to Emmetsburg from Parkersburg looked like a scene from the movie *Hoosiers*. Snow swept across the road on a cold north wind. The two team buses were nearly silent for the entire drive. A few players later said the trip felt like it would never end. To a man, everyone on the team knew they would eventually have to beat Emmetsburg; they just hoped that the game would come in the state finals in the UNI Dome, not in Emmetsburg on a snowy Friday night.

The players filed off the bus and went into the locker room to get ready for warm-ups. Ed went out on the field, alone. With no one around, he walked back and forth across the field where his team would soon play. *Lord*, he prayed, *I understand that it will take a miracle for us to pull this out tonight. I want you to know that whatever your will is, that's the way it will be. I accept that, Lord. I accept it.*

He joined his team in the locker room. Looking around the room, he could tell some of his players were scared. Others were on edge at the thought of knowing that the season could end tonight. "Fellas, it doesn't get any better than this," he said with a smile. "Eight teams left in the state of Iowa; two of the richest traditional programs in the history of football in the state playing each other for the first time. This is just another night we get to play this game. It's another night we get to go out and prove ourselves. Like I told you all week, it all comes down to who is going to come out and hit whom.

"We're not intimidated by coming to this place," he said with so much conviction that the players who were intimidated felt a little less scared. "And they wouldn't be if they came into our place. We've just got to block and tackle and be relentless for four quarters. For four quarters we've gotta keep coming. And remember, fellas, we are not going to face any more adversity out there than we've already been through.

"Tonight, guys, is about your legacy. That's what this program is all about. Where we are tonight has been passed down to you from those who wore this uniform before you. And you're going to pass this tradition down to the next group. That's what this is all about.

"All I ask from you tonight is to leave all you've got out on that field. And when we line up and shake hands after the game is over, we will look back on this with no regrets because we left it all out there. You're going to make memories tonight, just like you have all season. Now I don't know how this season will end, but let me tell you, whenever it ends, I don't want anyone to cry because we lost. Cry instead because the season is over, because this has been a season to remember forever.

"One of the papers here in Emmetsburg said tonight's game matches two evenly matched teams. They said the difference will be E'Hawk pride. I agree. We are two evenly matched teams. We mirror one another in a lot of ways. But the difference tonight is going to be FALCON PRIDE! I want you to go out there and enjoy every minute of tonight and compete your tails off! Let's go!"

On one of the first plays of the game, Falcon defensive back Coy Wiegmann ran over to tackle Emmetsburg's biggest running back. The collision left Coy lying flat on the ground. He looked up, snow falling through his face mask. He later said he'd never been that cold in his life. Nearly everyone else on the team thought the same thing. A damp cold hung over the field. Even so, A-P fought hard. Midway through the second quarter, with both teams scoreless, the Falcons drove to the Emmetsburg one yard line. The team that averaged 48 points per game in the regular season was kept out of the end zone for four straight plays. Emmetsburg took over and proceeded to move the ball slowly, methodically, down the field for the go-ahead touchdown. The first half ended with A-P trailing 7 to 0.

Emmetsburg extended its lead to 14 to 0 early in the third quarter. They were driving again midway through the fourth quarter when A-P recovered a fumble at its own twenty-five yard line. It appeared to be the break they needed. A-P came back to score a touchdown in the fourth quarter, although the two-point conversion attempt failed. They trailed 14 to 6 with less than five minutes to go in the game. No one on the Parkersburg sideline panicked. They had trailed with less than five minutes to go the previous Monday night and came back to win that game.

The Falcons forced an Emmetsburg punt on the ensuing possession. They took over the ball deep in their own territory with the clock winding down. Ed called a pass play, which should have taken the E'Hawks by surprise. A-P had been and would always be a running team under Ed Thomas. Emmetsburg was not fooled. They sacked Alec Thompson for a ten-yard loss. A screen pass to Alex Hornbuckle went for no gain on second down. Another pass on third down gained six yards, setting up a fourth down with fourteen yards to go. A minute and forty-seven seconds remained in the game.

Ed called a pass play down the left sideline to their horse, Alex Hornbuckle. Alex had gained over a thousand yards on the season as a running back. Unfortunately, the ball fell to the ground, incomplete. The emotional ride that began with Ed's bold pronouncement the day after the tornado was now over. The number one ranked A-P Falcons fell to the number two ranked Emmetsburg E'Hawks 14 to 6. Two weeks later, Emmetsburg won the state championship game.

Tears filled the A-P sideline as the clock wound down to 00:00. "Get your heads up," Ed told his players. "Get your heads up because you have nothing to be ashamed of. There were two great football teams out there tonight, and we came up short. But we've had a tremendous season. We are not going to hang our heads. We are going to walk off with our heads up!"

As the players made their way to the locker room, a reporter stuck a microphone in Ed's face. "Coach, this has to hurt," he said.

"It does, but this was a season I'll never forget. It has been a tremendous last five months for us, and I couldn't be prouder of our kids and the way they handled themselves tonight. They gave everything they had on the field, and you can't ask for anything more than that.

"I just feel bad that it's over."

Ed's senior picture in his high school letter jacket.

Ed stretching before track practice.

Ed and Jan leave for their honeymoon (1976).

Ed, Jan, Aaron in front of their church (1979).

Ed, Jan, Aaron, and Todd at the wedding of Ed's brother Greg (1991).

Ed as an assistant coach in the Iowa Shrine Bowl (1982).

Aaron as a senior,
Ed, and Todd
as a sophomore.

Ed and Jan at the Super
Bowl in Detroit after Ed is
named the 2005 NFL High
School Coach of the Year.

Ed mowing the
Sacred Acre.

Night game at the
Sacred Acre in
November 2005.

© Doyle Voss, Voss Studio Inc.

Ed talks on his new cell
phone while cleaning up
after the tornado.

Photo by Justin Hayworth, © 2008, The Des Moines
Register and Tribune Company. Reprinted by permission.

Photo courtesy of the City of Parkersburg

Aerial photo showing the path of tornado (from left to right).
The small circle identifies the Thomas home; the large circle
identifies Aplington-Parkersburg High School.

Aplington-Parkersburg football players work to clear debris from the football field in Parkersburg.

Aplington-Parkersburg senior Billy Aukes taps his helmet on the "Win Every Day" sign as he leaves the practice field Thursday night, just twenty-four hours before he and his teammates take to the field for the first time in the 2008 season.

Ed leads the Aplington-Parkersburg football team onto the field for their first home game after the tornado.

Ed with longtime assistant coach Al Kerns on the sidelines during a game.

Todd Thomas with longtime assistant coach and defensive coordinator Jon Wiegmann and Ed on the sidelines during a game.

Ed with his team and members of national media at the conclusion of the first home game after the tornado.

Ed and Jan in Hawaii on their first family vacation in twenty-five years (June 2009).

Ed teaching at a football camp at Dallas Center–Grimes High School.

At a press conference at Parkersburg Elementary School, Aaron Thomas speaks on behalf of the family about the shooting of Coach Ed Thomas, Wednesday, June 24, 2009. Also in the photo are special agent Jeff Jacobson, and Aaron's wife, Ellie Thomas.

Ed's casket is carried into First Congregational Church in Parkersburg before the funeral service on Monday morning. Helping as pallbearers are four NFL players who played for Coach Thomas. In the foreground (left to right) are Casey Wiegmann, Aaron Kampman, and Jared DeVries. In the background (third from left) is Brad Meester.

The casket is transported to Oak Hill Cemetery in Parkersburg on Monday morning after the funeral service. Hundreds of people line the streets leading into the cemetery to say good-bye to Coach Thomas.

The cover of *Sports Illustrated*, July 6, 2009.

Aaron, Jan, and Todd after receiving the Arthur Ashe Award for Courage at the ESPN ESPY awards on July 14, 2010.

CHAPTER 14

THE FIRST FAMILY VACATION (EVER)

I once had a person tell me,
"Thomas, you are the luckiest man I know."
I just smiled and inside said, "Thank you, God."
ED THOMAS

LIFE DID NOT SLOW DOWN FOR ED AFTER THE 2008 FOOT-
ball season ended. He found himself busier than ever with school
duties and with the design of the new gym, wrestling room, weight
room, and locker rooms. Like the outdoor facilities, he wanted to
make the gym state-of-the art, with a seating capacity of at least
two thousand. He had an ulterior motive. As Ed laid out his plans
for the gym, he did it with the hope that someday he could persuade
Aaron to move back to Parkersburg and take over as A-P's athletic
director and basketball coach. Ed wanted to have his son nearby,
but more than that, he wanted to someday coach his grandsons,
just as he had coached his sons.

One evening in early December, Jan interrupted Ed's planning
sessions and announced, "We're going on a family vacation. I'm
going to set it up. If ever we needed to get away, now is the time."

Truer words had never been spoken. Ed and Jan had not taken a vacation since their honeymoon. From time to time, they would talk about taking one, but somehow a trip never quite worked out. Early on in their marriage, they did not have the money to travel. Whatever extra cash they could scrape together from living on one income went into adding on to their eight-hundred-square-foot house to make room for their growing family. Once Aaron and Todd got a little older, the Thomases' travel budget went into trips that had them following their sons' traveling sports teams all across Iowa and surrounding states.

When the boys went off to college, money got even tighter. Ed and Jan's travel schedule squeezed out any room for a vacation. During Aaron's four years at Drake University, Ed and Jan went to as many of his games as they could, including making four trips to St. Louis for Missouri Valley Conference tournaments. They also made many quick trips to watch Todd play college football for Wartburg College. Because those trips came in the middle of Ed's busiest season, he always had to get back as quickly as possible. Jan ended up driving, while Ed worked on plans for his next game in the passenger seat. Stopping for dinner meant pulling up to the drive-through window at a fast-food restaurant.

The one trip that came the closest to qualifying as a vacation resulted from one of the greatest highlights of Ed's coaching career: the National Football League named Ed the 2005 High School Coach of the Year. Part of his award was an all-expenses paid trip for two to the Super Bowl, courtesy of the NFL. As soon as she heard where the Super Bowl was being played that year, Jan knew that this, too, would not rise to the level of a vacation. Most years, the Super Bowl is played in warm places like Miami, New Orleans, or San Diego. Not in 2006. Ed and Jan received a free trip to *Detroit*. In January.

None of that mattered to Ed. He had become more and more of a homebody as he got older, but he jumped at the chance to attend the Super Bowl. The League presented him with his award at a banquet a day or two before the big game. There he found himself in the same room as legendary players like Peyton Manning, Franco Harris, and Joe Namath. Ed even got to visit with then NFL Commissioner Paul Tagliabue. Kansas City Chiefs founder and owner Lamar Hunt introduced himself to Ed and Jan. Casey Wiegmann was the starting center for the Chiefs at that time. "Anytime you want to come to Kansas City to watch Casey play, you just let me know," Mr. Hunt told Ed. "You can sit in my seats anytime you want." Ed never took him up on his offer.

There was, however, one other perk to winning this award that Ed did accept. In addition to the plaque and the trip to the Super Bowl, the NFL gave Ed a cash prize. He had received a smaller cash award from the NFL when he was a finalist in 2003. He didn't keep any of that money for himself. Instead he poured it back into the A-P football program, just as he did the money he received for conducting coaching clinics and football camps. However, after he was nominated the first time, he promised his family that if he ever won, he would take everyone to Hawaii.

When Ellie heard that Ed won the award, her first words to her father-in-law were, "Woohoo! I guess this means you're taking all of us to Hawaii?"

"Uh, yeah, I guess I did say that, didn't I," Ed stammered. Only then did it hit him how far Hawaii was from Parkersburg. Before that moment, he had never worried about traveling so far because he never ever expected to win the award.

Jan wasn't nearly as hesitant. She went to work figuring out how to make the trip happen.

Finding the right time for the trip was a challenge. They could not go at any time between mid-July and the end of November because of football. From October through March, Aaron had basketball. March through the end of May did not work either because of both Ed's and Aaron's teaching schedules. That left summer. The summer of 2006 conflicted with football camps Ed had already scheduled. Jan decided to book the trip for June 2007. She ordered the plane tickets, booked the hotel, and set up their itinerary. Since she was booking the trip over a year in advance, it seemed like a good idea to her to buy trip insurance, just in case. She was glad she did when Ellie called one day and said, "I have good news and bad news. Which do you want to hear first?"

"I don't know," Jan said, "I guess the bad."

"Aaron and I can't go to Hawaii with the family," she said. "But the good news is, you're going to be a grandmother again!" Jan and Ed gladly traded a trip for the joy of welcoming another grandson.

Jan rescheduled the trip for the following June, as in June 2008, the month after the EF5 tornado. "You kids go ahead and go without us," Jan told Aaron and Todd, but they wouldn't hear of it. Jan canceled that trip too.

When Jan called the travel agent in December to set up the trip for June 2009, she was determined that nothing, not even another tornado, would make her cancel it. She made all the reservations and then called Aaron and Todd with the same message: We're going to Hawaii, and this time we mean it!

For most people, the point of a vacation is to get away to relax and unwind. Ed wasn't most people. He and Jan were excited about spending time with Aaron and Ellie and Todd and Candice, but Ed wasn't so sure about the relaxing part. That became clear the moment they arrived at Des Moines International Airport. Ed approached the trip like one of his practices, where every minute was planned and accounted for. "All right, everybody," he said, "let's get to the gate." He glanced at his watch. "It's already 8:10. We need to hurry up and get there."

"Ed, look at the clock up there. It's barely after 8:00. Your watch is fast," Ellie said.

"Nope, Eli." He always called her Eli instead of Ellie. "My watch is the official time for this trip." He took off toward the gate. Everyone else rolled their eyes and lagged behind. No one was late for the plane.

Once they arrived in Hawaii, the family headed straight for the beach. "You know, Ed, we should get you some sandals or flip-flops to wear out on the beach," Jan said to him. "You would be much more comfortable."

"My tennis shoes and socks will be fine," Ed said. "I don't really plan on getting in the water anyway."

"But, Ed, all that sand will get down into your shoes."

"I'll be all right."

True to form, Ed went out onto the beach dressed like he did every summer day in Parkersburg, with one exception. He had traded in his A-P ball cap for a light blue, cotton fishing hat with a short brim that ran all the way around. He wasn't exactly dressed for the beach, but he didn't care, and neither did anyone else. He walked over close to the water, and then, when a big wave hit, he nearly ran over the family trying to keep his feet dry. When he finally sat down, he turned to Aaron. "So, Aaron, are you relaxed?"

"Yeah, Dad. This is nice. Sitting here on the beach with the whole family. It feels pretty good."

"Hmm. Todd, you relaxing? Do you feel any different?"

"Of course," Todd replied. "My cell phone's not ringing. No one is e-mailing me with questions about their finances. Work is the last thing on my mind. So, yeah, I find this relaxing."

Ed gave a slight grin. "How about you, Ellie? Is this relaxing to you?"

"Yeah, Ed, that's the point of a vacation," she said.

"It is? This is what a vacation is about? This is what I am supposed to do? I don't feel any different than I do at home."

"Give it a chance, Ed," Ellie said.

Jan added, "If you would take your shoes off and maybe get into the water, you might just have some fun."

"Well, the five of you can do just that. I think I'll find a shady spot and do a little reading." He moved over to a spot under a tree and took out a book while everyone else splashed around in the ocean. Ed wasn't much of a swimmer. Growing up, he had never learned how. Jan convinced him to take lessons with Todd and

Aaron when they were young, "so you'll know what to do if you happen to fall in the pool." He learned just enough to keep himself from drowning, but he didn't much care for the water. Instead, he was content to sit in the shade and read.

Over the next several days, the six Thomases did all the touristy things one is supposed to do on Maui. On the second or third day, they went for a hike through a bamboo forest on the Pipiwai Trail in Haleakala National Park. "All right, follow me," Ed declared at the start.

Jan chuckled. "So, Ed, when did you learn so much about hiking trails in Hawaii?"

Aaron chimed in. "I think it was about the same time he became an expert on the New York subway system. He was giving complete strangers directions when we were in New York last year."

Ed turned around, grinned, and kept going.

"Come on, Ed, slow down. Enjoy all the nature around us," Ellie said.

"But that couple in front of us is pulling away," he said.

"This isn't a race," Ellie replied.

The next day, the family went to Pearl Harbor. Ed did not race through the exhibits and memorials. He paused at every historical marker and took it all in. Standing at the USS *Arizona* Memorial, he leaned over to Todd and said softly, "This is why we're here. We needed to see this." From there they went on a tour of the USS *Missouri*. "Right here is the spot where Hirohito and MacArthur signed the surrender document that ended the war," he said, beaming from ear to ear. "You know, I've taught history for over thirty years. Teaching it and seeing it are two different things. Boy, I'm glad we came here."

◆ ◆ ◆

Later in the week, Jan, Ellie, and Candice wanted to take a helicopter tour of the island. Ed, Aaron, and Todd decided that would be the perfect time to go play golf. Through the years, playing golf together had become their favorite way to spend time together. To an outsider, these may not have appeared to be friendly little games. The three of them went back and forth, needling each other on every hole. Today was no exception. Ed teed off first. His drive went right down the middle of the fairway. "That's how it's done, boys. That's how it's done."

"Really, Dad?" Todd said. "Hmm. Looks to me like that's just a warm-up shot. Let me show you what a tee shot is supposed to look like." Todd then proceeded to rocket his ball thirty yards past his father's. "Now *that's* how it's done."

Ed laughed. "I'd be worried if you couldn't outdrive a fifty-eight-year-old man, as big as *you* are. Just remember what they say —*drive for show, putt for dough.*"

"You two are nuts," Aaron said as he teed off. He was every bit as competitive as his father and brother. However, between raising three young sons, coaching basketball, teaching school, and serving as athletic director at Union High School in La Porte City, he didn't have the kind of time to play golf that his little brother and father had.

Walking off a green after putting out, Ed turned to his sons and asked, "So, are you guys having a good time? Has this been a good trip?"

"The best, Dad. Thanks for bringing us here," Aaron said.

"Wouldn't trade it for anything," Todd said.

"Good," Ed said. "I'm glad to hear it." Then he added, "You feel any different here than you do at home?"

"Of course," Todd said. "You?"

"No, not really."

Aaron smiled. "It's OK to relax and have a good time, Dad."

"I'm having a great time," Ed said. "Life doesn't get any better than playing golf with my two boys. But we could do this in Parkersburg."

Todd shook his head, laughing. "Everyone else in America

dreams of coming to Hawaii. You come to Hawaii and dream of going back to Iowa."

They finished their round. Todd beat his father by nine strokes, and his brother by thirteen, a small fact he made sure to mention several times during the rest of the evening. On their way back to the hotel, they stopped and grabbed something to eat. Ed ordered a hamburger, well done, with fries. "You know, Dad, you've basically had the same thing to eat every day since we've been here," Aaron said. "You can get a hamburger and fries back home. Why don't you try some of the local food?"

"I haven't had a hamburger every day. Yesterday when we went on that tour to that place called Hana, I had a hot dog."

Aaron just shook his head. Ed enjoyed his hamburger and fries.

On their last full day on vacation, Jan finally talked Ed into getting into the water. He pulled off his Nikes and socks and waded out about waist deep. A wave broke around him. "Wow," he shouted, "can you believe that undertow? Feels like that wave might drag me out into the middle of the Pacific."

"I don't think it can budge a stick-in-the-mud like you," Ellie joked.

"Hey, you have fun your way, and I'll have fun my way, Eli," Ed said.

"I'm just glad we finally got you in the water. I can't imagine coming all the way to Hawaii and never once getting in the ocean," Ellie said.

"No," Ed said with a smile, "neither could I."

"So, do you feel relaxed yet, Ed?"

Ed just grinned.

CHAPTER 15

AN ORDINARY DAY

Success in life is a peace within,
knowing you are working to be the man or
woman that God has called you to be.
ED THOMAS

Tuesday, June 23, 2009, was hot before the sun even came up—hot *and* humid. A few early-morning thunderstorms rolled through, but the rain did nothing to help with the heat and only amped up the humidity levels. By 9:00 a.m., the heat was nearly unbearable, but that didn't stop forty of Coach Scott Heitland's football players from Dallas Center-Grimes High School from showing up for a football lineman clinic. When Scott was a college student, Ed hired him to coach the ninth grade football team at A-P. The next year, Scott did his student teaching under Ed. Once he graduated from college and became a head coach on his own, Scott asked Ed to do a day camp just so that his players could be around Ed Thomas. Ed was more than happy to do it. He tried to do camps for all of his former coaches who had gone on to take head coaching positions.

Scott's offensive linemen looked forward to the camp every year. When he first arrived at Dallas Center-Grimes five years earlier, Scott had to sell the camp to his team to get them to show up. Not anymore. The first year, players came because the new coach wanted them to and because it was an opportunity to learn from a man who had taught four players who now started in the NFL. Now they came because they loved being around Ed Thomas. It was the high point of the summer for Scott's team.

"Well, Scott, looks like you've got a pretty good group out here today," Ed said as he arrived. On this particular day, Ed brought along several of his assistant coaches and former players. Ed's brother, Greg, came over from Humboldt, Iowa to help. Like his big brother, Greg became a football coach. In 2006, his team won Iowa's class 3A state title. He joined Ed in these camps every chance he got. Even though the two were eighteen years apart, they were close.

"Yeah, Coach, we do. It should be a great day," Scott replied.

"Now you keep an eye on your guys for me. I don't want them to get overheated. If you think we need an extra break, you let me know."

"Of course I will, Coach," Scott said.

Scott called his players together and introduced Ed.

"All right, fellas," Ed started in, "I know a lot of you have been with me before. I appreciate your coming out here on such a hot day. Over the next couple of hours I want to show you a few of the things we do over in Parkersburg that we've had some success with over the years. I'm not telling you it's the only way or the right way, but it has worked pretty good for us. Now you juniors and seniors, a lot of this may be pretty basic for you, but that's OK. I've been doing this a lot of years, and I find that you win or lose based on how you do the little things. If you do the small things well, the big things will take care of themselves.

"The first thing I want to show you is the proper way to do a three-point stance." As Ed continued to speak, he got down into a three-point stance himself. He shifted around a few times, demonstrating the wrong way to do the stance and the bad things that can happen if you mess it up. Then he shifted into a correct stance and took off as if the ball had just been snapped.

"All right, fellas. It's your turn." As players went through their drills, Ed paced around them. "Good job there. Hey, buddy, what's your name?"

"Jimmy Smith, Coach."

"Yeah, Jimmy, I remember you from last year. You've bulked up a lot since then."

"Yes, sir."

"What does your daddy do for a living, Jimmy?"

"He works for the county, Coach."

"He does, does he? I tell you what, Butler County over where I live could use some good men to come to work for them. You ought to move over there and come play for me. Whaddya say, Heit?" he said to Scott. "Whaddya think about Jimmy here coming over to play for my Falcons?"

"I don't think so, Coach. You're not getting your hands on this one."

"You're doing a good job there, Jimmy," Ed said as he patted the kid of the back. "Keep it up. You've got a really good coach here."

The player beamed. Every player on the field that morning knew this was the coach who had four linemen in the National Football League. Whenever Ed singled out a player in the camp and said he wanted him to come play for A-P, he made that player feel like he had what it took to go far in football.

During the first morning break, the players jogged over to a shady spot to get some water to drink. Ed walked over to his brother, who had found a place to sit down under a tree on the far side of the field. "I want to ask you something," Ed said.

"Sure. Anything," Greg replied.

"You need to tell me when I can't do this the way I need to do it. If you see I'm not getting through to the kids and getting them to give it all they've got, you tell me. No one else will. The day I stop getting through to them is the day I need to get out."

"Of course I'll tell you. You know I'll be straight with you. But I don't think you have to worry. These boys today—they're listening.

When they saw you fire off the line and dive into that blocking dummy, let me tell you, you got through to them, especially on a day like today."

"Thanks, Greg. You know, I figure I can go another fifteen years and coach all my grandsons," Ed said with a smile. "That's the plan anyway."

"I think you'll get there," Greg said. The conversation trailed off, and Ed went over to speak to some of the other coaches. Greg watched Ed walk away. From the time he was a little boy, he had always admired his big brother as the kind of man he hoped he could be. With their age difference, Ed was almost like a second father when Greg was growing up. Once Greg graduated from college and started coaching himself, their relationship became more like the siblings they were. Like any brothers, they were fiercely competitive with one another. They played golf on Greg's wedding day, but Ed didn't let up on him. He beat his little brother by two strokes.

Greg never felt any pressure from being Ed Thomas's little brother, as if his brother's shadow kept him from being able to shine. Instead he counted himself lucky to have Ed as a brother. Greg sought out Ed's advice constantly—from how to handle certain game situations to which job he should take. The one thing he admired about his brother above all else was Ed's peace with his calling and mission in life. Their mother had once told Greg that she had always prayed that Ed would become a preacher, not a football coach. He told her, "Mom, Ed is changing more lives doing what he's doing than he could ever do as a pastor. He preaches every day in the way he coaches and teaches." To Greg, Ed understood his role on this earth more than anyone he had ever met.

"Hey, Greg," Ed called over to him, "you ready to start back, or are you going to take a nap over there?"

"I'm coming," Greg said as he got up and jogged over to the rest of the coaches.

✦ ✦ ✦

"Hi, uh, can someone help me?" It was the voice of a person Jan did not recognize. He leaned over the counter of the newly rebuilt city hall. "Wow, it feels good in here. Hotter than blazes outside."

"Yes. Air conditioning sure is nice. What can I do for you?" Jan asked.

The man reached into his pocket. "I found this lying next to Highway 57 over near the ice cream place," he said as he laid a card on the counter. "I figure it was from the high-speed chase Saturday night. You hear about that? Can't believe he didn't hit anyone when he came flying through town at ninety miles an hour. I figure he must have thrown it out the window to keep the police from figuring out who he was."

Jan picked up the card. It was a driver's license. "I appreciate you dropping this by."

"You know who it was, don't you?" the man asked.

The question struck Jan as rather odd since she had the driver's license right in front of her.

"Mark Becker," the man continued. "Good thing he hit that deer instead of a person. That's a wild way for a high-speed chase to end. But you know, you always gotta be careful around here. Deer are thick this time of year."

"Yes, they are. Well, I appreciate you bringing this in. I'll take care of it," Jan said. As soon as the man left, Jan picked up the phone and called Joan Becker. The two had been friends nearly as long as Jan and Ed had lived in Parkersburg. Joan and her husband, Dave, had been members of Ed's Sunday school class since he started it back in the late 1970s. Back then, it had been a young marrieds class, since everyone in the class, including Ed and Jan, were young and newly married. Now it was more like the middle-aged married-forever class.

"Hi, Joan, this is Jan. Hey listen, someone just brought in Mark's driver's license."

"Thanks," Joan replied. "I'll come by and pick it up."

Jan hung up the phone and looked at the license. Dave and

Joan's middle son, Mark, had played for Ed for four years, including during the 2001 state championship season. In the years since Mark had graduated, Ed kept in contact with him. Whenever he saw him at church, and those occasions were becoming more and more rare, Ed always tried to encourage Mark to do the right thing and to make good choices. "Mark, you've got your whole life in front of you," Ed said to him time after time. "It doesn't matter what's happened so far. You've made a few mistakes, but that's OK. You can turn it around. I know you can."

Unfortunately, the talks didn't seem to have done much good. Joan regularly requested prayer for Mark during Sunday school. Most Sundays, Ed was the one who prayed aloud for Mark. Neither Ed nor Jan knew the details of what had gone on with Mark since he graduated from high school, nor did they need to. They just knew that Dave and Joan had been through a rough time with him.

A short time later, Joan Becker came into city hall. "Hi, Jan, I appreciate you calling."

"I knew Mark would need his license, and you are probably the best person to get it to him," Jan said.

"I guess so. I suppose you heard he was in the high-speed chase that came through town Saturday," Joan said.

"I did. It is a small town, you know." Jan didn't see the chase herself, but Aaron and Ellie had. They were in town for Father's Day weekend. They had walked over to the local ice cream shop when a car flew by, with Chris Luhring's car and a couple of Butler County sheriff's cars close behind.

"It is that. After the chase they took Mark to Covenant Hospital." Joan let out a sigh of relief. "We've tried to get him to go for a while now, but he didn't want to. But now he's there, finally. I think he'll finally get the help he needs and get on the right meds for his mental illness." She paused for a few moments to catch her breath. "I'm so glad he's finally in a place where he can get some help. He should be there for a while."

"I'm glad to hear it, Joan," Jan said. Jan knew Mark had struggled with drug abuse in the past, but this was the first time Joan had mentioned Mark's mental illness to her. Joan did not elaborate as to the nature of his illness, and Jan did not think it was any of her business to probe further. "You know Ed and I pray for Mark all the time, and for you and Dave. We'll pray that this works," Jan added.

"Thanks, Jan."

Joan took Mark's driver license and left. Jan went back to work. Later that night, she and Ed prayed for Mark, just as Jan told Joan they would.

During the lunch break at the offensive lineman camp, Scott Heitland invited Ed and the rest of the coaches to his house to eat. His house had a large basement that had been converted into living space, which is where he served lunch. It was the coolest spot in the house. After eating, Ed found a spot on a sofa where he leaned back and fell asleep. Through the years Ed had established a reputation as someone who could nap anywhere and everywhere. Once or twice he had caught some heat for nodding off during faculty meetings. A few minutes before 1:00, he jumped up off the couch, wide-awake, and said, "All right, let's go." Scott shook his head in amazement. Even asleep, Ed stuck to his schedule.

At the close of the afternoon camp session, Ed asked all the players to take a seat on a grass berm on one end of the practice field. More than any of the techniques Ed taught, this end-of-camp talk was the primary reason Scott had Ed do football camps every year. "Now, fellas, we've had a pretty good camp today in spite of the heat. You all worked hard out there, and I appreciate that, and I know Coach Heitland appreciates it as well. Like I told you, the techniques you learned today are not necessarily the only way to do things, but they've worked for me through the years. Now, if your coach tells you to do things different, you listen to him and do what he says. He knows what's best for ya."

Scott smiled at that line. He appreciated Ed deferring to him, but he needn't worry about a conflict in their techniques. Since coming to Dallas Center-Grimes High School, Scott patterned most of his line drills after those he learned as an assistant coach under Ed. In fact, he already used nearly every drill and technique Ed went over on that day. That was another reason he had Ed come in for the camp. During his practices, Scott would bark things like, "Coach Thomas would be embarrassed if he saw you get off the ball like that. Line up and do it again." Or, "There you go. That's the way to do it. That's exactly the way Coach Thomas showed you back in June."

"You know, guys, I've been doing this for a lot of years, for thirty-seven years, to be exact. And I have to tell you that my fire and commitment and enthusiasm for this game are stronger today than they've ever been. I don't know how many more years I'll get to do this, but I plan on making the most of every one of them.

"And that's what I want to challenge you young people with today, especially you seniors. Make the most of this opportunity you have to play this game, to leave a legacy. You see, this is about more than the game of football. The way you choose to practice, the way you choose to play each game, the way you choose to devote yourselves to giving your all every play of every game for four full quarters—all of that says a lot about how you will choose to live the rest of your lives.

"Every day that you get up out of bed, every day God gives you on this earth, is an opportunity for you. He gives you each day to do with it whatever you want. You can waste it, or you can use it for good. Just remember, what you choose to do with each day is very important because you are exchanging a day of your life for it, and you don't know how many days you will have. When tomorrow comes, today will be gone forever. All you will have is whatever you traded this day for.

"You know, I believe the greatest gift God has given any of us is the power to choose. That's what you get to do with every day you get to spend on this earth. You get to choose how you're going to use it. I don't know about you, but I want to choose to use each day for gain, not for loss. I want to choose good, not evil. I want to choose whatever is going to help me succeed and be a better person and make a positive impact on the lives of others, rather than choose things that lead to failure.

"The future is just a long string of right nows.

"I've found that football and life really aren't that complicated. You always get out of it what you put into it. When you make good decisions on and off the field and choose to work hard and do your very best, no matter what you are doing, good things happen. And when you make a mistake and blow it, and goodness knows I've made a lot of mistakes through the years, you get back up off the ground and learn from it.

"All right, fellas, thanks for coming out today. Heit, you got anything you want to add?"

"No, Coach. I think you said it all," Scott said.

CHAPTER 16

THE UNTHINKABLE, JUNE 24, 2009

I want to finish the race
with God working through me.
ED THOMAS

"BUTLER COUNTY 911."

"We, uh, had, a, I think, a shooting right now in the bus barn down at the high school." Daryl Myers struggled to keep his composure as he spoke into his cell phone. To the dispatcher he sounded very calm, very much in control, but he was anything but. Daryl could not believe the words coming out of his mouth. He felt like he was about to throw up. *This cannot be happening*, he thought.

"Yeah, at the high school where?" the dispatcher asked.

"Uh, in the bus barn."

"In the bus barn?"

"Yeah, yeah," Daryl said as high school students raced past him, running for cover. He noticed one adult running toward the bus barn. Daryl recognized him as one of the parents who had dropped off their kids earlier. A few minutes earlier, the man had been sitting in his car, reading the paper, waiting for his daughter to finish lifting weights in the bus barn that was serving as the weight room. Now he ran toward the bus barn while everyone else was running away from it.

"Do you know who it was?"

"No I don't, uh," Daryl said, "kids just came running out and said somebody shot Ed Thomas."

"Ed Tho ..." The dispatcher gasped and tried to catch her breath. Finally she managed to spit out, "OK."

Daryl had been in the bus barn himself maybe ten minutes earlier. He had gone in with vital news to share with Ed. "Your sod is in," Daryl told him.

"Great," Ed replied. "That spot over by the visitors' stands still looks pretty bad.

"We can get on it right after you're finished here, if you want."

"I should be through in about an hour."

"All right. I'll have everything ready to go when you are." Daryl turned to walk out. Off to one side sat the orange lawn mower Ed used to mow the field. The sight of him on that mower was one of the staples of life in Parkersburg. As he walked out of the weight room, Daryl overheard Ed talking with one of his football players: "Way to go! Good job. That's a new personal record for you, isn't it?"

Standing outside the bus barn a few minutes before 8:00 a.m., surrounded by panicked students, waiting for the police to arrive, Daryl could not believe what was happening. He dropped his cell phone into his pocket and raced toward the bus barn. "Go, go, go," he called to students running past him. "Get down there," he said, pointing to the elementary school across the street from the bus barn.

At 7:53 a.m., Chris Luhring's pager came to life. "Shots fired at the high school." Like every town in America, Parkersburg had its share of crime, mainly drugs, but the town hadn't seen a murder since sometime in the 1920s. As police chief, Chris did his best to keep it that way. Even though this was his day off, the moment he read the words "shots fired," he ran to his bedroom, changed out of his pajama shorts, threw on a shirt, and headed toward the door.

"Chris, wait! You don't have your vest," his wife yelled, referring to his bulletproof vest. She had taken it apart to wash it earlier that morning.

He scooped up his weapon, handcuffs, and radio and shouted back, "I don't have time to put it back together. I have to go NOW!"

"But, Chris," she said as he dashed out the front door and into the white Ford Explorer that served as his squad car.

He shot out of his driveway and headed toward the school, lights flashing, siren blaring. "1223 Butler County," he said into his radio, "1223 Butler County." No one responded. The emergency radio system went down right after the call went out about the shooting at the high school. Chris pressed down harder on the gas pedal, his speedometer climbing to sixty as he flew through the neighborhood near the school. "1223 Butler County!" he shouted into the radio, but still no response. "Crap!" he yelled and threw the microphone aside.

The moment he turned the corner onto Johnson Street, he saw kids running. He pulled into the school parking lot. The lot was always busy with construction traffic. The school was scheduled to reopen in less than two months.

Before Chris could get out of his car, kids ran over to him, hysterical. Two screaming voices overpowered all the rest. "Coach has been shot! Someone shot Coach Thomas!"

Chris shook his head, trying to make sense of what he had just heard. "WHAT!?"

"He shot Coach in the head!"

"Who shot him?"

"Some guy. You've got to help Coach!"

"Does anyone know the shooter's name?"

"No!" multiple voices scream.

"Did he leave the school? Did anyone see what he was driving?"

"He ran out the back of the building," one voice shouted.

"He left in a blue car," yelled another. "He drove off going north."

Chris jumped out of his squad car and pulled out his gun. The pounding of his heart echoed in his ears. He didn't know what to do first. He had to get these kids to a safe place, but he also needed to find the shooter. *Get to Coach! Get to Coach!* he screamed in his head. A trained EMT, he knew he had to get to Ed as quickly as possible to try to help him.

"Did he drive away or did he run out the back of the building?" Chris tried to put all the pieces together, while more information flew at him. Kids collapsed, weeping and wailing. Some kids screamed. Finally Chris grabbed one boy who seemed to know the most. "Here, take this paper and pen and write down everything you're trying to tell me. Go to that bus over there, and write it all down for me. I'm going to go check on Coach."

"I'm not gonna get in that bus!" the kid panicked. "No, it's not safe."

"Calm down, son," Chris said. "I'm here. I'll protect you."

"No. If I get in the bus, I'll be trapped."

"Fine," Chris said. "Go over on the far side of the bus, outside the bus, and write everything down for me. I'll be right back."

The throng of kids moved over toward the bus. Chris herded them along to a spot where he thought they would be safe. Only then did he race to the bus barn.

❖ ❖ ❖

Jan was just about to walk out the door to go to work when her EMT pager went off. "Parkersburg ambulance," the dispatcher said, "we have a gunshot/stab wound at the high school weight room." Jan looked at the clock on the wall. Ed normally called her every day around 8:00 after he finished in the weight room. She thought, *I should call him and ask what's going on.* Instead, she grabbed her purse and darted out the door.

"Sounds like one of the construction workers had a nail gun accident," Jan said. Climbing in her car, she pulled out her cell phone and called her boss. "Hi, Gary, I wanted to make sure you knew I've been called out with the ambulance, and I'll be a little late for work."

Jan drove the few blocks to the station, climbed into the ambulance, and waited for another EMT to respond to the page. Since most of their volunteers work outside of town, putting a crew together during the day can sometimes be a problem. The dispatcher set the tones off again, only this time adding the code 1033, which means EMERGENCY!

"Dispatch, this is Parkersburg ambulance." Jan wanted to tell the dispatcher to set off the tones again because she didn't have a crew. Dispatch never answered. For some reason the radios were down. Jan used her cell phone to call and told the dispatcher to start an ambulance crew from Aplington. If this truly were a 1033, they needed to get a crew there as soon as possible. Jan was about to give up on any other help arriving when two other crew members pulled into the fire station parking lot.

"All right, let's go. You drive," she said to one of them. The other EMT climbed into the back. Jan called the dispatcher on her cell phone and said, "We're en route."

The fire station was less than a half mile from the high school. Jan got her kit ready so she could get to work the moment they arrived.

◆ ◆ ◆

Chris walked in the weight room door. Two men cradled Ed as he lay on the floor. The weight room equipment partially obstructed his view, but Chris could see enough. One of the men looked up at Chris, obviously in shock. "It's real bad, Chris. Really bad. I don't know what to do."

The policeman in Chris fought to keep him in control. Chris the former Falcon football player, Chris the man who admired Ed Thomas more than anyone on earth, Chris who counted Ed as his best friend, wanted to run over and grab hold of Ed and not let him go. He pushed his emotions down, but he felt he was about to lose the battle. "Just stay with him. Help should be here soon," he said.

A siren started off in the distance. *Oh, my gosh, Jan is on her way*. Chris knew she was in the ambulance because she was always the first to respond when the ambulance was called out, especially during the day. As this thought ran through Chris's mind, he stepped closer to Ed. Blood from the head injury seemed to obstruct Ed's breathing. "All right, we need to turn Coach onto his side. Keep him off his back and on his side, OK?"

Chris took one last look at Ed. Ed's breathing was labored, but he was still alive. "Hey, Coach, everything's going to be all right. I want you to know that. Hang in there. The ambulance is going to be here real quick and you'll be all right." Ed didn't respond, but Chris thought he heard him. *Oh my, he's lost so much blood*, he thought to himself but didn't dare say it out loud.

"I've got to secure the scene," Chris said and jumped up. "Stay with him, guys. Keep talking to him. I'll be right back." As soon as Chris came to a spot where Ed could not hear him, he called his dispatcher on his cell phone. "Dispatch, I need you to get the air ambulance started this way. We need it here RIGHT NOW!" He paused for just a moment as his knees buckled. "Keep it together, Chris," he told himself, "keep it together."

The students had told Chris that the shooter took off out the back door of the weight room, so Chris dashed off in that direction, gun drawn. Pushing through the door, he did a quick, frantic search of the parking lot. If the shooter was still here, Chris was fully prepared to use deadly force. He looked for the car the students described. It was nowhere to be found. A handful of cars littered the parking lot, but all of them were empty. Every student, as well as all the parents and anyone else on school grounds, had scattered over to the elementary school.

"Chris, is the scene safe?" someone called out to him. He looked up and saw the ambulance stopped at the parking lot entrance.

"Yes," he called back. "Pull in and park directly in front of the doors of the bus barn. I'll meet you there."

As the ambulance turned in front of Chris, he saw Jan sitting in the passenger seat. The moment it stopped, the three EMTs jumped out, Jan in the lead.

Chris jumped in front of her. "Jan, stay right here with me," Chris said.

As one of the EMTs took off running into the bus barn, Jan tried to follow her. "No, Jan. Stop!" Chris yelled out.

"I need to get in there," Jan said. She tried to get around him.

Chris grabbed her by the shoulders. "Jan, stop."

"I don't understand," she said.

"Jan, look at me. Listen." Chris swallowed hard. Tears welled up in his eyes. "The person in there is—it's Ed, Jan. He's been shot several times in the head."

Those words did not make sense to Jan. This was supposed to be a workplace accident involving a construction worker and a nail gun. "How is he?" she said.

"It's bad, Jan. It's very, very bad."

This is impossible. This is impossible. This is impossible. "None of this makes any sense, Chris. It can't be Ed. This was a construction accident, right?" Her mind could not comprehend what she had just heard. It sounded impossible.

"No, Jan. Someone shot Ed with a gun."

Jan began to tremble from head to toe. "I need to get to him. He needs me."

"I don't want you to go in there. Not yet, at least. Your crew has to do their work, and you know they can't do that with family right there."

"OK," she said in a near whisper. She fought to keep from hyperventilating. Shock swept over her. *Oh, God, what has happened?*

The pain in Jan's face was nearly more than Chris could bear. *Ed knows she's here*, he thought. *He had to have heard the siren. He must know she is here. How can I keep her outside when he knows she's here.* He pushed those thoughts away as hard as he could. His years on the ambulance service taught him that grieving family members get in the way of the medics. And Ed needed medical attention right now more than he needed his wife. *Please, God, let him be all right.*

More ambulance crew members arrived and went inside to help. Jan stood with Chris outside. Time seemed to stand still for her. Every second outside was sheer torture, wondering how he was, praying she would walk inside and find him lying there with a smile on his face, then telling her he was embarrassed by so many people making a fuss over him.

"How are you holding up?" Chris asked.

Jan nodded and tried to say, "I'm OK." The words stuck in her throat. By all rights she should have been in hysterics. Inside she was, but somehow she kept it together on the outside. Finally, she leaned over to Chris and said, "I need to go in, now. I know what you told me. I know it's bad. But I need to go in there now."

"OK," Chris said without trying to talk her out of it. "When you go in there, you need to tell him that everything is going to be all right. He needs to hear your voice. He needs to know you're here."

Jan nodded and headed toward the door.

The EMTs were loading Ed onto a backboard when Jan walked in. The local pastor who rushed in when the kids ran out was still at Ed's side, praying over him. Jan walked over and knelt down beside Ed. For a split second she was able to take in the scene as a paramedic rather than the victim's wife. She did a quick survey of his wounds. Right away she knew that he probably would not survive, although she did not allow her mind to process that thought. He didn't appear to be conscious, which did not surprise her, given the extent of the injuries she could see right in front of her.

"Ed, I'm here," she said. The moment those words came out of her mouth, the EMT in her melted away. She took hold of his hand. Tears streamed down her face. "I'm here. Everything is going to be all right. They're going to take good care of you." *Please, God, let him be all right.* She held tightly to his hand and did not want to let it go. Ever. But her EMT training kicked back in, and she knew she needed to get out of everyone's way as they fought to stabilize him and prepare him to be transported to the hospital. "I need to step away so the guys here can help you. I love you, Ed. I love you."

She stepped back and looked around at her friends with whom she had worked together on many, many serious accidents. The looks in their eyes confirmed what she already knew. *No, no, no, no. Oh, God, no,* she cried inside as outwardly she kept her composure. "Thanks, guys, for everything." Her voice cracked ever so slightly as she dismissed herself.

Jan walked out of that room and into another room inside the bus barn where she could be alone. She pulled out her cell phone and dialed Aaron's number.

"Hey, Mom, what's up?" Aaron said as he answered the phone. He and the high school principal at Union High in La Porte City were on their way to an administrative conference in Des Moines. They were nearly there.

"Aaron, there's been an incident at the high school. Your father has been shot, and it doesn't look very good." Jan could barely force herself to say the words.

"What? What do you mean he's been shot, Mom? Dad doesn't have a gun. He doesn't hunt. How could he be shot?"

"No, Aaron, this wasn't an accident." She paused to try to gain her composure. Part of her wished she had asked Chris to make this phone call, but she felt she needed to be the one to break the news to Aaron. She pushed the words out with all her strength. Even then, they barely came. "Someone shot your father several times. It's bad, Aaron; it's really bad."

"Where are you, Mom? Is anyone with you?" Panic welled up in Aaron's voice.

"I'm still at the school with the ambulance crew. They are getting ready to transport your dad, I think to Covenant Medical Center in Waterloo. Chris is here with me. He called for the helicopter, so they may take your dad to University Hospital in Iowa City. I'll let you know."

"You're serious, aren't you? This is really happening?"

Jan's voice broke as her grief and pain poured out. "I am afraid so. Would you call Ellie and see if she can get hold of Todd? I don't have the contact information for the hotel where he and Candice are staying in Jamaica." Todd and Candice were in Jamaica for a friend's wedding.

"Sure, Mom. Anything." Aaron hung up the phone, and turned to his principal. The look on his face said everything. He blinked hard and rubbed his head. His mother's words rang in his ears. Aaron felt like he had just stepped into someone else's nightmare. "We need to turn around. Someone shot my dad."

"What? Who?"

"They don't know," Aaron said, but one name leaped into his mind.

At church in Parkersburg that Sunday, someone had started talking about the high-speed chase that had come through Parkersburg, a chase that began in Cedar Falls, twenty miles away. That was when Aaron found out that Mark Becker had been the driver. He also learned why the police were chasing him. Apparently, Becker had attacked a house, trying to get to the people inside. He bashed in the windows with a baseball bat and then grabbed a tire iron and tried to break down a door. All the while, he screamed profanities at the top of his lungs and threatened the people inside. When he could not break through the doors with the tire iron, he jumped into his car and tried to drive it through the garage door. About that time, he heard police sirens and took off. The police chased him all the way from Cedar Falls through Parkersburg and out toward his grandparents' house. The chase ended when Becker hit a deer seven miles outside of Parkersburg. Chris Luhring was the arresting officer.

Aaron had never understood his father's commitment to Mark, especially since he had done so many things that went against everything his father stood for. Ed told Aaron the same thing he had told Todd about Mark. Aaron could still hear his father say how Mark needed the team more than the team needed him and that he would not give up on him. And now this. Aaron did not yet know who shot his dad, but the more he thought about it, the more he knew only one person was capable of it.

The principal turned his truck around and headed toward Parkersburg. A Gulf War veteran who had led his unit into Baghdad, he knew what it was like to lose someone very close to him. He patted Aaron on the leg and drove without saying a word. He gave Aaron space to grieve. They were at least two hours away. Aaron called Ellie and broke the news to her. She tried to call Todd and Candice in Jamaica, and then broke down in tears, unable to move or speak.

✦ ✦ ✦

Chris paced in front of the bus barn. The air ambulance helicopter was still at least fifteen minutes away. *We have no time! We've got to get him to the hospital NOW!* But Chris wasn't sure he could leave the scene. He thought the shooter was gone, but he didn't know for sure. At any moment, more shots could fly from God knew where. Panic tried to set in. He looked over at Jan. The color had drained completely from her face. *She can't ride in the ambulance, and she sure isn't in any condition to drive herself. Where is that HELICOPTER?!*

His cell phone chimed, telling him he had a text. It read, "12-1 and 12-2 have the shooter in custody." 12-1 was the Butler County sheriff; 12-2 his deputy.

That settled it. "All right, let's get rolling," Chris yelled to the ambulance crew. He called the dispatcher on his cell phone. "Have the air ambulance contact me when they get close. I need them to meet us on the way." Then he turned to Jan. "Ride with me, OK?"

Jan nodded. She then followed behind as the EMTs rolled the gurney to the ambulance. A friend put his arm on her shoulder and whispered something in her ear. She didn't hear him. Right before they loaded Ed into the ambulance, she took his hand and said, "They're taking you to the hospital now. It's going to be all right.

I'll be right behind you. I love you." As she released his hand, she feared these would be the last words she would ever say to him. The crew lifted up the gurney. Jan stood off to one side, softly crying. She tried to pray for her husband, but she did not know what to say.

The ambulance doors slammed shut, pulling Jan out of her daze. The ambulance took off, siren blaring. Jan climbed into the passenger seat of Chris's squad car, the same Explorer that had nearly been destroyed during the tornado a year earlier. Before he got in the car, Chris grabbed Dave Meyer, the high school principal. "Lock the bus barn up tight, and don't let anyone go in or out. It's a crime scene." He then took off behind the ambulance, lights flashing, siren blaring.

They weren't even out of the parking lot when Jan looked at Chris and said, "Those are mortal wounds, Chris. I want to pray for him, but I don't know if I can pray that he survives this. The shots in the head ..." Her voice trailed off. "If he survives he will not be the same, and Ed would never want that."

"Jan, we're both medics. We've both seen some very bad stuff where it looks like there is no hope, and the people make a full recovery. Remember that woman who was dead, but you and I brought her back with CPR? Don't give up." Chris was telling himself this as much as Jan. As an EMT himself, he knew Ed's chances were slim at best.

The ambulance sped south down Highway 14. The air ambulance got through to Chris's radio. Whatever was wrong with the radio system, it had to be in Parkersburg, not on Chris's end. He set up a rendezvous point on Highway 20, a four-lane divided, limited access highway near the town of Dike. Dike is halfway between Parkersburg and Cedar Falls/Waterloo. Chris and the ambulance carrying Ed reached the point first, which allowed Chris to stop traffic and set up the landing zone for the helicopter. Once the helicopter landed, Chris told Jan, "You probably have time to check on him before they take off."

"OK," Jan said. There wasn't room for her to climb into the

helicopter and sit down next to Ed. Instead, she opened the door and looked in. Her husband's eyes told her what she was afraid she already knew: He would not recover from these wounds and probably would not survive the trip to the hospital. She took a deep breath and whispered, "I love you."

While Jan spoke to Ed, Chris answered a phone call. It was Butler County Sheriff Jason Johnson. "We've got him in custody, the shooter. You know who it is, don't you?"

"I have no clue," Chris replied.

"Mark Becker. It is Mark Becker."

"Can't be. They locked him up in the psych ward. The hospital was supposed to notify us when he was ready to be released so we could put him back in jail."

"Yeah, I know, but they didn't. It's Becker all right. I'm staring at him right now."

The doors of the helicopter closed. The medic on board took over Ed's care. Chris and Jan climbed back into the squad car and took off toward Covenant Medical Center. "They have the shooter in custody, and you might as well know who it is because you are going to find out pretty quickly," Chris said.

Jan took a deep breath.

"Who?"

"Mark Becker."

"That's impossible. Joan told me yesterday that he was in the hospital and that they were going to keep him for a while."

Chris shook his head. He felt like vomiting. "I'm sorry, Jan, but that's who it is. They're questioning him right now."

Jan could not respond. She and Chris rode in silence the rest of the way to the hospital. When they arrived, Chris pulled around to the emergency entrance in the back.

The helicopter landing pad was nearby. It was empty. They had beaten the helicopter to the hospital. Jan prepared herself for the worst that she knew was coming.

CHAPTER 17

A NIGHTMARE
UNFOLDS

*Being a Christian does not mean we will
always win and be exempt from adversity,
disappointments in life, and problems.
Being a Christian is hard.*
ED THOMAS

TODD WAS JUST ABOUT TO SIT DOWN TO EAT AN OMELET WHEN
he noticed Candice running into the hotel restaurant, her hand over
her mouth. She had woken nauseated, so Todd assumed Candice
had her hand over her mouth to keep from throwing up. Getting sick
away from home is always rough, and waking up sick in Jamaica is
even worse. Candice stopped at the restaurant doorway and looked
around. As soon as she spotted Todd, she sprinted over to him.

"Ellie's on the phone. You need to talk to her," Candice said.

Todd could see his wife was very upset. "OK," Todd said. "Why?
What's going on?" He was more than a little surprised anyone had
called. With no cell service for his phone on the island, he hadn't
heard from anyone back home since they arrived two days earlier.

"Someone shot Dad."

Todd assumed Ellie meant someone had shot Candice's dad.
"What? Why would someone shoot your dad?"

177

"No, you don't understand. Someone shot *your* dad. Someone shot Ed." She burst out crying.

That statement made even less sense to Todd. "He doesn't hunt. How could he get shot?" He pushed his plate away, and he and Candice took off running toward their room. The television was on CNN when he walked into the room.

Todd grabbed the phone. "What's going on, Ellie?" he asked his sister-in-law. He glanced over at the television. "That's Jon Thompson," he said to himself as he saw the A-P superintendent on the television screen.

"Someone shot your dad. It looks really bad. Everyone's been trying to get ahold of you to let you know."

The banner at the bottom of the screen read, "Coach Ed Thomas Shot." Jon Thompson was live, speaking at a press conference about what had happened.

"What? I mean, how did this happen?" Todd said.

"Apparently someone came into the weight room this morning and shot him."

Todd stepped back. His knees gave way, and he dropped to the bed. "Do they know who did it?" Tears filled his eyes.

"I think they have someone in custody."

Todd rubbed his head and tried to force his mind to process what he had just been told. "Where is Dad now? Which hospital did they take him to?"

"Covenant. I'm going to head over there as soon as I can get someone to watch the boys."

"But he's going to be all right, right?"

Ellie did not answer. After a long pause, her voice cracked, and she said, "You need to come home as fast as you can."

Tears flowed down Todd's face. "All right." His heart raced. The room seemed to spin. On the television in front of him, CNN's coverage of the Parkersburg press conference continued. Candice lay on the bed, clutching a pillow to her chest, sobbing. "I don't know how quickly we can get a flight out of here," Todd told Ellie.

"Let me check on it. As soon as you know something more, let us know."

"I will."

Todd hung up the phone and stared at the scene in his hometown on the TV screen. A feeling of helplessness swept over him —helplessness and fear. Candice came over and wrapped her arms around him. The two sobbed and prayed. Local time was just after 9:00 a.m. Over an hour had gone by since the shooting.

◆ ◆ ◆

"This way, Mrs. Thomas," the hospital official said to Jan as she came into the emergency room area of Covenant Medical Center. "We have a room set aside for you right over here. Reporters and camera crews have already started pouring in, but we're keeping them in another part of the hospital. Just let me know if you need anything."

"Thank you," Jan said. She walked into the waiting room. The new associate pastor from her church, Phillip Jensen, was already there. He had been on the job for less than two weeks, and this was his first staff position. The senior pastor was on vacation, which left Pastor Phil to fill the role of chief comforter. His eyes were red from crying when he looked up at Jan.

When Jan walked in, Pastor Phil got up and hugged her. "Everything is going to be all right," he whispered to her.

Jan knew better. She closed her eyes, and the image of Ed lying on the floor of the weight room flashed through her mind. She opened her eyes quickly. *How can this be happening?* The pastor opened his mouth as if he was about to ask a question, but he stopped himself. Instead, he patted her on the back and began to weep. Jan could not cry. The tears would not come, but they would soon.

Chris waited outside with a hospital paramedic near the helicopter landing pad. Overhead came the sound of the chopper getting close. "What the heck is that guy doing?" the paramedic said as he pointed toward a reporter on the other side of the road. The newsman held a camera with a telescopic lens. Clearly, he thought he had himself in the perfect position to capture images of Ed Thomas coming off the helicopter.

Chris took off across the street, furious. He jumped over a fence and planted himself right in front of the reporter. "What are you doing?" he yelled. The rage that had built up from the moment he walked into the weight room and saw his best friend lying on the floor in a pool of blood now came roaring to the surface. The reporter mumbled something about snapping shots of the air ambulance, as if his photos had nothing to do with the passenger aboard this particular helicopter. Chris wouldn't hear of it. "If you snap even one picture, I will see that you live to regret it!" Chris warned. The newsman backed away but did not leave.

Chris turned to see the helicopter touching down. Jeff Jacobson, the Division of Criminal Investigation (DCI) special agent in charge of the case, had notified Chris to stay with Ed at all times. Because this was a criminal investigation, anything removed from Ed had to be collected as possible evidence, even down to something as insignificant as his watch. Chris dashed back across the street as an EMT placed Ed's stretcher onto a gurney. One of the nurses climbed up onto the gurney and started chest compressions. Chris assumed they had been performing CPR in the helicopter since the moment they picked Ed up out on Highway 20.

The emergency room supervisor found Jan in the waiting room as the helicopter landed. Jan's face was in her hands. *Oh, God, I don't know how to pray. I want you to save my husband, but I can't be selfish. Please don't keep him alive just for me, not if that means he will never get out of a hospital bed again and never be himself. He would never want that.*

"Excuse me, Mrs. Thomas," the ER supervisor interrupted Jan and said, "We just brought your husband in. They've started CPR and are working on him right now. I'll have one of the doctors come in to talk to you as soon as they can."

"All right," Jan said. "Thank you." Now she understood why she and Chris beat the helicopter to the hospital. She knew from her EMT training that the helicopter could not take off until Ed was stabilized. Jan thought he must have crashed right after the helicopter doors closed. They must have started CPR right after she last spoke to Ed.

Jan sat still for just a moment and then stood up. "You know what?" she said, "I need to go back there and talk to the doctors now."

"Excuse me?" the ER supervisor said.

"I need to talk to the doctors so they can be clear on what my husband wants."

"All right, Mrs. Thomas. Follow me."

The ER supervisor stepped inside the curtain where a team of doctors and nurses was working on Ed. A moment later, Jan stepped inside the curtain as well. Ed lay on the table, tubes and wires running off in every direction. One of the attending physicians continued doing CPR compressions on him. Chris stood off to one side, keeping a close eye on everything but making sure to stay out of the medical team's way. The primary physician looked up at Jan.

"I appreciate everything you're doing to save my husband's life, but please don't continue if he has no hope of a viable recovery," Jan said. "Over the years, Ed made it clear that he did not want to be placed on life support and kept in a vegetative state."

"We won't, Mrs. Thomas. We won't. We still have a couple of things to check. Then I'll come out and give you an update on his condition."

"Thank you, doctor." Jan stepped outside the curtain and paused for just a moment. *Father ...*, she prayed.

Jan went back into the waiting room. More friends and family had arrived during the short time she was talking to the doctor. All wept openly. Several came over to Jan, hugged her, and said the kinds of things people say in hospital waiting rooms. The words and the faces all ran together for Jan.

A few minutes later, the doctor walked into the waiting room. "I'm sorry, Mrs. Thomas," he said, "we did all that we could. I am afraid your husband has passed." The grief that had been building in the room as everyone waited for the inevitable came pouring out.

Jan took a deep breath. "Thank you, doctor, for all you did for my husband."

"I'm very sorry for your loss," the doctor said. "In just a few minutes, you'll be able to come back to see him."

"Thank you," she said in a voice just louder than a whisper. She fell back into her chair, more numb from shock than anything else. The pastor came over and prayed with her. Friends sat next to her and put their arms around her. Most were crying too hard to speak. Jan's mind could not wrap itself around the fact that this was really happening. "Excuse me," she said to those gathered around her. "I need to call Aaron."

Jan stepped out of the room and dialed her son's number.

"Hi, Mom," Aaron said with a very cautious tone. He was afraid to hear what was coming next.

"Aaron ..." She paused, trying to gather the will to force the words out. "Your father didn't make it."

"Are you OK, Mom?" he asked.

"Yeah, I'm doing OK."

"Ellie should be there soon."

"Good ... good."

"I'll call her and tell her. I'll have her call Todd."

"Thank you, Aaron." Jan knew that emotionally she couldn't make any more calls. "Would you call your Uncle Greg too?"

"Sure, Mom, whatever you need."

"Be careful driving over here."

"I will, Mom. And, Mom ..."

"Yes."

"I love you."

"I love you too, Aaron."

Jan had just hung up the phone with Aaron when a nurse stepped around the corner and said, "You can come back now, Mrs. Thomas."

"OK." Jan followed the nurse into the trauma room where just a few minutes earlier doctors fought to save Ed's life. She took a deep breath and then stepped inside.

✦ ✦ ✦

"Should we go ahead and try to book a flight home, or wait until we hear something?" Todd asked Candice. Getting a flight out of Jamaica at the last minute was easier said than done. "I wonder if we can even get a flight out today?" He paused and tried to gather himself. "I don't know what to do. I can't believe this is happening."

"I can't either." By this point, Candice had already started throwing things in their suitcases. "We should probably go ahead and see if we can get out of here today. You know we'll go nuts if we don't."

Todd let out a long sigh. "Yeah. I'll go downstairs and see if the concierge can help. Stay here in case Ellie calls back."

Downstairs, one of the hotel staff members was able to get through to the travel agent who had booked Todd and Candice's trip. The agent changed their reservation and was able to get them two seats on the next flight out of Kingston. It also happened to be the last flight out for the day.

Back upstairs, Todd called Ellie on the room phone. "Have you heard any news?" he asked. "How's Dad?"

Ellie could hardly speak. "I'm sorry, Todd. He didn't make it."

Todd broke under the news. Candice held on tightly to him.

"I'm at the hospital now," Ellie said.

Todd struggled to gain his composure. "Is my mom there close by? Can I speak with her?"

Todd and Jan talked for a few minutes, carrying on a conversation neither of them could believe they had to have. At the end,

Todd said, "We're about to leave for the airport. We'll be home as quickly as we can, Mom."

Friends and family began filling the waiting area. The media could not get back to where Jan was, but everyone who came to see her had to go through the gauntlet in the hospital lobby. Ellie was one of the first to arrive. A few minutes later, Al and Deb Kerns came in. Al had coached with Ed since 1978. Through the years, Jan and Deb had become very close friends. In their younger days, they had a reputation for doing some crazy things. Back during the 1980 season, when what was then only Parkersburg High School first played for the state championship, Jan and Deb disguised themselves as superfans, complete with masks, and invaded the football team pep rallies. They appeared out of nowhere, like two phantoms, and proceeded to work the crowd into a frenzy. Then, just as suddenly, they disappeared. Neither Ed nor Al, nor any of the coaches, knew who these phantom crusaders might be. They might never have known if Ed hadn't stumbled across their costumes while digging around in the attic one evening while Jan and Deb were out bowling.

Jan was sitting with her arm around Ellie when Al and Deb walked in. As soon as Deb saw Jan, she broke down sobbing. Jan walked over, wrapped her arms around her friend, and held her for a very long time. "It'll be OK," Jan whispered. "He was hurt so badly that if he had survived he wouldn't have been Ed." As Deb struggled to pull herself together, she found it more than a little ironic that she had come here to comfort Jan, but Jan was the one doing the comforting.

Several of Ed's close friends came into the family waiting room, including the guys Ed met for coffee most mornings. The press clamored for a statement from the family, but Jan didn't want to say anything until after Aaron arrived. Jan phoned him again. He was supposed to arrive at any time. In the meantime, at least thirty people filled the waiting room. A television was on in one corner. The game show that was on was suddenly preempted by a special report. There on the screen came the words, "COACH ED THOMAS HAS BEEN MURDERED." The room fell silent. No one felt like talking anymore.

◆ ◆ ◆

Todd and Candice arrived at the airport with very little time to catch their flight. They grabbed their few bags and checked in as quickly as possible. Normally, before they could board the plane bound for the United States, they would have to go through customs, but neither was taking anything out of the country. Even so, the process took up precious time they did not have. As they walked up to the customs officials, Todd tried to explain their situation. "We don't have much time. This is an emergency, and we booked these tickets home at the last minute."

Candice, standing nearby, tears flowing, finally pointed at the television nearby where CNN carried live coverage of the Ed Thomas story. "That's our father, OK? We *have* to get back."

Customs officials dispensed with the usual inspections. Todd signed a waiver, and he and Candice took off toward their gate.

When they touched down in Miami, Todd turned on his cell phone. It lit up with voice mails and text messages, more than he could count. He and Candice were scheduled to fly from Miami to Minneapolis, with a long layover. However, one of the text messages came from Aaron Kampman, telling Todd that he and Candice had tickets on a direct flight to Cedar Rapids that left in just over an hour. Unfortunately, that plane had mechanical issues, and the flight was canceled. Aaron called Todd and told him he had lined up a private jet that could fly down to Miami to pick them up. However, this plan fell apart because of storms rolling through the Midwest. Aaron then arranged for a jet to meet them in Minneapolis, but the same storms ruled that out as well.

For five hours, Todd and Candice were stuck in the Miami airport. Everywhere they went, televisions blared, every single one tuned into CNN. People around them went on about their business.

Children laughed; couples bickered; a middle-aged guy a few seats down took a nap. Above them all, CNN broadcast hourly reports from Parkersburg with continual updates into the investigation of the shooting of the beloved Coach Ed Thomas. Todd and Candice tried to keep themselves together as best they could. No one had any idea who they were or how much each news report hurt them.

Finally, they boarded a plane to Minneapolis. It was the closest they could get to Parkersburg, due to the odd combination of bad weather and mechanical problems on airplanes. Mike and Nancy Brannon, Candice's parents, made the two-hundred-mile drive north to meet them and drive them home. Eighteen hours after the shooting, Todd and Candice arrived back in Parkersburg.

◆ ◆ ◆

While Todd and Candice were at the Jamaica airport, Aaron arrived at Covenant Hospital. Jan had instructed him to come around through the ER entrance to avoid the throngs of reporters and television cameras in the main lobby of the hospital. His principal ran interference for him as they walked through the parking lot and into the hospital. If anyone had had any ideas about running up to Coach Thomas's son, the principal was there to make sure it did not happen.

Once Aaron finally made it to the family waiting room, Ellie was the first person he saw. She ran over, and the two wept together. "Where's Mom?" he asked after a few moments.

"Over here," Ellie said.

Aaron walked into a small room off to the right side of the main room, where a crowd of family and friends had gathered. He wrapped his arms around his mother and held on to her. Neither said a word for a very long time. Finally, Jan asked, "Do you want to see him?"

"Yes," Aaron said.

Jan led Aaron and Ellie back to the same trauma room where medics had brought Ed when the helicopter transported him to

the hospital. Aaron walked in. The breathing tube was still in his
father's mouth, although it was no longer connected to the machin-
ery. He saw the gunshot wounds on his father's head and the evidence in the room of how the doctors had fought to save his dad's
life. At the head of the bed stood Chris Luhring. He didn't say
anything at first. Instead he moved back away from Ed to give the
family plenty of room.

Aaron walked over closer. "Why are there bruises on Dad's
chest and head?" No one had an answer.

Ellie stood back to one side as Aaron walked over and said
good-bye to his father. Jan took him by the hand. The two stood
there silently, weeping, unable to believe this had really happened.

Before Aaron, Ellie, and Jan left the room, Chris spoke up. After
telling Aaron how sorry he was and how much Ed meant to him,
Chris asked the question he knew he had to ask but did not want
to. "Aaron, do you want to know who did this?"

"Yes, of course."

"It was Mark Becker."

Aaron did not say a word, but anger flashed in his eyes.

Once the Thomases left the trauma room, Chris called DCI to
tell them that Ed's body could be released to the coroner. After the
hospital staff took custody of Ed, Chris excused himself and found
an empty room down the hall. There he let loose all the emotions
he had held in since he walked into the high school weight room
and saw Ed on the ground. It wasn't just the loss, as great as it was.
Chris fought with himself over the fact that Mark Becker was even
on the streets. *Why didn't anyone tell us they were releasing him
from the hospital? We asked to be notified. Why didn't anyone
call? If someone had called us, if anyone had said they were letting
Mark Becker out, he would be in jail right now, and the best man
I've ever known in my life would be alive!*

Chris left the hospital a short time later to go back to Parkersburg and get to work on the worst case of his life.

◆ ◆ ◆

Later that afternoon, back in Parkersburg, the Thomas family agreed to make a statement to the press. The press conference was to be held in the makeshift DCI headquarters that had been set up in one of the portable buildings at the elementary school. Right outside sat the practice field on which Ed had spent innumerable hours working with young men. Across the street sat the Sacred Acre. And below that was the bus barn he had pushed so hard to build the summer before so that his team would have a locker room for the football season that followed the tornado. Earlier in the day, Jon Thompson had formally announced Ed's passing to a large group of reporters. A sports anchor from Waterloo who had covered the A-P Falcons throughout his career, broke down weeping, as did several other reporters.

Throughout the day, reporters crawled all over Parkersburg, each one looking for some sort of scoop. Vans from stations across Iowa had set up shop in the school parking lot. Camera crews interviewed anyone and everyone they could. Reporters nearly went into a feeding frenzy when cars transporting family members pulled up to the elementary school.

Ed's brother, Greg, and his wife, Michelle, accompanied Aaron and Ellie to the press conference. DCI agents, along with local police officers and sheriff's deputies, filled the room. As they walked into the portable classroom, a woman came in right behind them. Aaron turned around and noticed her walking right behind Greg. "What are you doing here?" he asked.

"I'm with him," she said and pointed to Aaron's uncle, Greg.

"No you're not," Aaron said. "He has a wife, and *you're* not it."

The woman was speechless. Apparently, she had come to town looking for a story. Now *she* was one. A DCI agent promptly escorted her out of the building.

Once order was restored, Aaron walked up to a podium. Television cameras from across the state and the country were in front of

him. "Obviously with the shocking events today, nothing can prepare you for what our family and community are going through,"
Aaron began. "Many of you knew my father as a teacher and as a
coach. I think the part that gets overlooked and the thing that he
was most proud of was his involvement in the church as an elder at
First Congregational Church in Parkersburg. He was a man of deep
faith who touched many lives not just on the football field. But the
thing he talked about most was making people better young men.
And also with all the students he had. So I guess that is one thing
that as a family we would really like to come out.

"I know on behalf of my brother and myself, my wife, all my
dad's brothers and sisters, my mom's brothers and sisters as well,
our family thanks everyone for the thoughts, the prayers, the concern for our family. We especially thank the people of Parkersburg
for their devotion to our family, for all the overwhelming support
during this tragedy, for the many phone calls and visits we have
already received. In the midst of our grief, we are greatly apprecia-
tive of our friends and neighbors and the community of Parkersburg and the school of A-P for all they've done for us."

Then Aaron said something that shocked the reporters covering
the story. He said, "We also want to make sure we express our concern and our compassion for the Becker family. We ask that people
pray for them as well and that people take time to comfort and be
with them through this as they are also going through a lot."

He concluded by talking about the impact his father made on
his own life and the entire community. "God always has a reason,"
he said. "At this time it is very tough for us to understand that."

After asking the press to respect his family's privacy, Aaron
brought his remarks to an end without taking any questions.*

❖ ❖ ❖

---

*For video of the June 24, 2009, press conference, go to *www.youtube.com/watch
?v=cqONlFliaNo.*

When Jan arrived home from the hospital, she found that city workers had blocked off her street. Work crews had popped off all the manhole covers, and a city truck and trailer set up barricades to make it appear as though they were working on the city sewers. Aaron stopped his car at the barricade, and Jan called out, "Do I have water?"

The worker smiled. "Of course. Don't worry. This isn't real. We just didn't want any reporters or anyone else to be able to get too close to you."

Even so, a crowd was waiting at home for her. Never in her wildest dreams could Jan have imagined something like this happening to her family.

CHAPTER 18

GRIEF AND GRACE

*Whatever you do in life
echoes thru eternity.*
ED THOMAS

PARKERSBURG WAS DARK AND QUIET WHEN TODD AND CAN-
dice pulled into town a little after 2:00 a.m. — that is, with the
exception of one house. Everyone in the Thomas household was
awake, waiting for them. No one would have been able to go to
sleep anyway. Awaiting Todd and Candice's return gave the family
something to think about besides funeral preparation and answering questions from the police conducting a murder investigation.
Once Todd and Candice arrived home, Todd was ready to stretch
his legs. At least that's the excuse he gave. He wanted some time
alone with his brother, just the two of them.

Aaron and Todd walked outside and headed straight for the
Sacred Acre. A few hours earlier, an estimated two thousand people
had filled the stadium for a prayer vigil for their father. The news
media called it an impromptu gathering, but that wasn't exactly
true. The local clergy pulled it together right after word spread that
morning of Ed's murder. People from as far away as Des Moines
filled the stands, covered the track, and sat on the hillsides around
the field. Choirs sang, preachers spoke, and the town wept. During
the vigil, Aaron and Ellie walked over near the Methodist church

that overlooks the field, just to have a look. They did not attend the vigil itself. They went out of their way to escape notice. No one in the family was ready to walk into the middle of a crowd and start answering questions.

Aaron and Todd didn't say much as they made the short walk from their parents' house to the school. In some ways, it reminded both of them of the day they made the same walk with their father right after the tornado. People in town had already started comparing the two disasters. More than one person said something like, "We were able to rebuild our house, but we'll never be able to replace Coach."

As they walked along, Aaron said, "I knew who did it the moment Mom told me Dad had been shot."

"How?" Todd asked.

Aaron proceeded to tell Todd about how Mark Becker used a tire iron and baseball bat to smash the windows and doors of a house in Cedar Falls while trying to get to the people inside, and the subsequent high-speed chase that came through town on Saturday. "Chris told me that since Becker had been arrested on a Class D felony, the hospital was supposed to notify either his office or the county sheriff before they let him out of the psych ward," Aaron said. "If they had, none of this would have happened. Dad would still be alive." Anger and grief filled his voice. "I mean, how can a hospital let someone dangerous back out on the street like that and not have to let anyone know? Chris said they claimed HIPAA* laws kept them from notifying his office. That's ridiculous. I don't know how, but we need to make sure this doesn't happen to anyone else."

Todd didn't say much in return at first. Mostly he took it all in, trying to sort through the grief and anger that swept over him. Todd is far more emotional, like his father, while Aaron is like his mother. Finally, Todd asked, "Do they know why he did it?"

Aaron shook his head. "I don't know. None of this makes any

---

*Health Insurance Portability and Accountability Act.

sense. All dad ever tried to do was help him out. And this is how Mark repays him."

Eventually the two came to the practice field that sat on a hill above the Sacred Acre. Students had taken red cups and shoved them into the chain-link fence. The sign read, "Coach T," followed by a heart. Below the sign, numerous people had left flowers, cards, and photographs in a makeshift memorial. The two brothers stood and stared at the memorial for a long time. The moment felt incredibly surreal.

"Did you get to see him before he died?" Todd asked.

Aaron shook his head. "No. I was in Ames on my way to Des Moines when it happened." In fact, the last time Aaron saw his father was three days before the shooting, on Father's Day. The two of them had gone out and done what they loved to do together more than anything else—play golf. Yet their round that day was very different, and not just because Aaron drained a birdie putt on the last hole and beat his father for the first time in a long time. Throughout the round, Ed had talked about what remained to be done at the school's athletic facilities. He gave Aaron very specific details about things no one else knew, including his plans to add a set of steps on the east side of the football field and his vision for what the unfinished ticket booths would look like. Ed gave Aaron a laundry list of projects and told him which fund to use for each project. At the time Aaron didn't think anything of it. Every time he came to Parkersburg his father gave him a tour of the under-construction school, pointing out details on the gym and weight room that he'd already pointed out a hundred times before. But now, looking back on the conversation after his father's death, to Aaron it seemed his dad knew his time on earth was short, and he wanted to make sure Aaron knew how to finish what Ed had started.

"When did you talk to him last?" Aaron asked Todd.

"Saturday night, before Candice and I left for Jamaica the next morning. I called to wish him a happy Father's Day. I played golf that morning and shot a pretty good score, so I wanted to let him know I would've bumped him pretty good if I had been home and played with the two of you." Todd paused for a moment. "The last thing I said to him was that I loved him. He said, 'I love you too, pal,' and hung up the way he always did without saying good-bye."

"Yeah, Dad never did have the best phone manners. Of course, I do the same thing." Neither one said much of anything after that. They walked from the practice field over to the high school parking lot. Their father's little red truck still sat exactly where he had left it when he arrived at school a little before 7:00 the previous morning. An Aplington police officer saw them approaching and jumped out of his car to stop them. However, he immediately recognized them and climbed back in his car without saying a word.

Aaron and Todd weren't sure what time they returned to their parents' house. By then, almost everyone had gone to bed. The house was quiet and dark. Aaron headed off to bed, while Todd walked the short distance to his in-laws' house, where Candice was already asleep.

❖ ❖ ❖

The sky had just turned light when Jan gave up on sleep. From the moment she learned Ed had been shot, she had not had one second alone. Everyone meant well, and she needed her family nearby, but she woke up feeling an intense need to be completely alone. She needed time to think and to process what had just happened.

More than anything, she needed time alone with God to pray. Not that she wasn't praying already. Over the previous twenty-one hours, she had stayed in a continual state of prayer. God's grace and strength were the only things that kept her from collapsing under the weight of grief, anger, and disbelief. Yet her prayers had been more cries for help than real conversations with God. Now she needed the latter. She needed to talk to God as she tried to come to grips with an act of cold-blooded evil that had robbed her of her husband and best friend.

She dressed quickly and quietly so as not to awaken Aaron and

Ellie, who were sleeping in the next room, and slipped outside. The city trucks remained in the middle of her street, barricades up, manhole covers off. The throng of reporters would return later in the day, but no one was standing outside with a camera and microphone at 5:00 in the morning.

Jan walked down her street and headed straight for the high school. No one was outside. For the most part, Parkersburg was still asleep. If this had been a normal Thursday, the football players would be up soon for their morning run. Ed had the team lift weights on Monday, Wednesday, and Friday and run on Tuesday, Thursday, and Saturday. But this Thursday was anything but normal. For Jan, normal no longer existed.

Why, God? she prayed. *Why? Why? Why? How does a man who never hurt a soul, a man who never even had a fistfight in his entire life, end up gunned down? All Ed ever wanted to do was help young people grow into the best men and women they could possibly be, and one of those young men into whom Ed poured his life ends up brutally murdering him right in front of the very kids he is trying to help? God, it doesn't make any sense.*

It is all too cruel.

Tears rolled down Jan's face as she walked. Soon she found herself in front of the practice field fence and the ever-expanding memorial there. Flowers covered the ground, along with cards, letters, and photographs. She picked up a few cards. One read, "Coach Thomas will be remembered as a man of great faith in God." Another read simply, "We love you, Coach." From the day she first agreed to go out on a date with Ed, she had always shared him with his work. But it wasn't really his job that took up so much of his time; that she never could have put up with. Reading these cards she was reminded again that what drove Ed was not his work but his mission and calling. All he wanted to do was make a difference in the lives of young people, and the notes on the cards were evidence that he had done just that. *But why did it have to end like this?* she prayed.

She leaned over and placed the cards back on the ground, back on the memorial. The next thing she knew, she was across the street, sitting in the stands of the football field. Like Ed, Jan never called this the Sacred Acre. A sign on the other side of the field read "Ed Thomas Field." She remembered how Ed had put up a fuss when the school told him they wanted to name the field after him. Now, sitting here, staring out at the field, his absence pressed on her, inflicting physical pain. *Why, God?* she prayed softly. *Why?*

God did not respond in an audible voice, yet he answered. Jan did not hear an answer to the question of why; yet in her spirit she heard God whisper the words of Romans 8:28: "And we know that in all things God works for the good of those who love him, who have been called according to his purpose." *In all things ... in all things ... in all things — even in a senseless murder.*

I am at work here, she sensed God say.

Looking out at the field, she began to realize that God had already been at work through all of Ed's years of coaching and teaching here. No one outside of the Aplington and Parkersburg areas should have ever heard of Ed Thomas. Yet on this field, God gave Ed the opportunity to coach four players who went on to play in the NFL, which led to Ed's receiving national attention and being named NFL High School Coach of the Year. Then, when the tornado hit, even more national media flooded into town to cover the story. The football team and Ed's leadership of the team became a centerpiece of the story line of the town's recovery. That gave Ed a platform both in the state of Iowa and around the country, where he was able to share his faith and talk about the grace of God and the power to choose that he gives us.

And now this, she prayed. *Can this possibly be part of the all things you work in?* As these thoughts swirled in Jan's head, Romans 8:28 grew louder and louder.

No act of evil can destroy my purpose and my plan, God whispered. *I'm still on my throne. I'm still God. This did not take me by surprise. Please trust me.*

Tears flowed down Jan's cheeks. *Is it as simple as that, God? Is that all I have to do—trust you—and everything will be all right? But you did not say everything would be all right. You said you would work in all things for the good of those who love you and are called according to your purpose. Oh, Lord, it hurts so bad, but I believe you will do what you say you will do. God, please take this act of evil and use it for something good.*

Jan stood up and looked back up the hill to the sign made out of red plastic cups stuck in the chain-link fence. A peace came over her, a peace that reassured her that Ed's work and influence had not come to an end at 8:00 a.m. the day before.

This realization did not answer her question of why Ed's life had to end so horrifically. Nor did it cause her pain and anger to suddenly disappear. Yet she knew she did not have to carry this burden herself.

The sun rose up over the horizon. A few cars moved down the street in front of the high school. Jan decided to return home before anyone noticed her. The house was starting to stir when she walked in the door. She and Aaron and Todd had so much to do today, making arrangements at the funeral home and planning the funeral itself. *Oh, God, I can't do this, but I know your grace and your strength are sufficient.*

Later that day, she went into her bedroom and closed her door behind her. She pulled out her cell phone and dialed a number her pastor had given her when the family met with him in the Thomases' home. The call went straight to voice mail. "Hi, Joan. It's Jan. I know we're both going through a really tough time right now. I wanted to tell you how sorry I am that it was Mark. I'm praying for you. Please call me when you get a chance."

CHAPTER 19

THE HARDEST PART

*As a father, there is nothing more important
than to see your family walking with God.*
ED THOMAS

JEFF JACOBSON HAD WORKED AS A POLICEMAN FOR A LONG time, but this was without a doubt the hardest duty he had ever pulled. Shortly after 8:00 on the morning of the shooting, the Butler County sheriff called Jeff as the special agent in charge of the Northeast Iowa Division of DCI. "I have Mark Becker at gunpoint," the sheriff said. "What do you want me to do with him?" From that moment on, Jeff was the officer in charge of the murder investigation, yet his connection to the case went much deeper. He wasn't just a special agent for the DCI who supervised difficult cases; he lived a few houses down from the Thomases in Parkersburg. Jeff and Ed had been friends for years, a friendship that grew when Jeff's sons played football for the A-P Falcons.

Jeff's personal connection to the Thomas family made his meeting with the family to explain what had happened to Ed the hardest thing he had ever had to do since becoming a policeman. Yet, because of his friendship with Ed, he felt like he needed to be the one to help break those details to Jan and Aaron and Todd.

On Friday afternoon, two days after Mark Becker shot Ed Thomas, Jeff sat down in a conference room at city hall with the family. "I want to say first off that our deepest sympathies are with you through this tragedy," he started off. "I thought the world of Ed and will miss him deeply." He paused to gather himself. If he allowed himself to think like a friend rather than a policeman, he would never get through this briefing.

"We wanted to bring you up-to-date on where we are in the investigation and brief you on what actually took place the day Ed was killed. Obviously, there will be some information we cannot divulge because of the pending trial, as well as some things we don't know but are still investigating. And if at any point you have a question, feel free to ask."

The Thomas family nodded that they were ready.

"I would like to introduce agent Jack Liao to you. Jack has been in the lead for much of the investigation. He will explain where we are and what we've learned so far." With that, Jeff sat down in a chair off to one side. He crossed his legs and lowered his head.

"From our interviews with Mark Becker, we learned he had been planning this for a couple of weeks," Jack said. "Apparently his anger with Ed, for whatever reason, had been building for some time, as far back as last September. We don't know why. A while back, he tore down a poster that hung in his parents' house that had Ed's picture on it. Becker had also ripped out Ed's eyes on the poster.

"On the day of the shooting, Becker got up early and went to breakfast with his father. He gave no indications of what he was planning. In fact, he talked about getting some help for his mental illness. Dave told us that he came away more optimistic about his son than he had been in a long time. Obviously, neither Dave nor Joan had any idea what their son was planning.

"After his parents left their house, Becker broke the padlock off a cabinet and removed a .22-caliber handgun. He then went outside and took target practice. He proceeded to Aplington in search of Coach. He told us that he had originally planned on killing the entire family but later changed his mind." The Thomas family looked at each other with shocked looks of disbelief.

Jack continued: "Becker went to a house near the middle school. A witness, an older woman, said he asked if the Thomases lived in this house. Given the number of people from Parkersburg who moved to Aplington after the tornado, either temporarily or permanently, that didn't strike us as completely odd. The woman told him no, and he got back in his car and left. The assistant principal at the middle school was the next person to encounter Becker in Aplington. Becker asked if he knew where Coach Thomas was. The assistant principal told him that Coach was probably at Parkersburg Elementary School teaching driver's ed.

"That's where he went next. One of the elementary school custodians said Becker came in and asked where Coach Thomas was because he wanted to do some work for Coach. The custodian made a couple of phone calls to track Coach down. He was the one who told Becker that Coach was in the weight room at the bus barn. Again, nothing about Becker's demeanor gave anyone a hint as to what he was really up to."

Jack paused and let out a long sigh. "Once he arrived at the high school, he walked over to the bus barn and stuck his head in the door for just a moment. He then returned a minute or two later and walked in the door, his hands down at his side. Ed was standing with one of the football players when Becker approached him. Coach said, 'Hey, Mark,' and then Becker raised a gun and fired the first round, striking Coach in the head."

The family fought hard to keep their composure. Candice buried her head into Todd's shoulder, while Ellie grasped hard onto Aaron's arm. Aaron put his other arm around his mother.

"Ed fell to the ground. Becker then continued to fire at him, for a total of seven shots."

Todd interrupted. "You're sure of where he shot my dad first? He wasn't shot in the knee or the stomach first? You're sure of that?" This question had haunted Todd since the day of the shooting. He could not bear the thought of his father suffering in great pain as he was shot repeatedly.

Jack looked around at his team. Jeff spoke up. "Yes, Todd, we are. All the witnesses confirm that the first shot was to the head at very close range. The boy who was standing next to your father said that Becker raised the gun very quickly and aimed it at the boy's head first. The boy shut his eyes, thinking he was about to die. He heard the gunfire and opened his eyes, and that's when he saw that your father had been shot in the head."

"A rumor is going around town that my dad jumped in front of one of the students to keep him from getting shot," Aaron said, "but it sounds like that's not what happened."

"No, it's not," Jack said.

"One more question," Aaron said. "My dad had some bruising on his face and on his chest when I saw him in the hospital. Do you have any idea how that happened? It doesn't seem like falling to the ground would do that."

Jack looked over at Chris, who dropped his head.

"Witnesses told us," Jack said, "that after Becker shot your dad he, uh . . . ," he took a deep breath before he went on to say, "he then stomped on your father, striking him multiple times in the face and in the chest and shouting profanities at him."

"He what?" Todd asked, his voice breaking with anger.

"He stomped on your father, shouting profanities at him," Jack said.

"After he was already down on the ground and could not defend himself at all?" Todd said. He swung his body around as if he had just been kicked in the chest. Candice wrapped her arms around him and whispered something in his ear.

"That is correct," Jack said.

"Could he . . . uh . . ." Todd fought to keep himself together. "Could my dad feel it?"

"No," Jack said. "We know he lost consciousness after the first shot, so there is no way he felt anything after that. He did not suffer pain."

Todd shook his head, fighting back tears. "Good . . . good."

"Did he say why he did it?" Aaron asked, his jaw clenched to keep his emotions in check.

"Mark clearly had some deep-seated animosity toward Ed, but we don't really know why he wanted to kill him. We are still trying to figure that out," Jack replied.

Aaron asked, "Where is he now?"

"He's at the county jail. We've already charged him with first-degree murder."

"What about bail?" Aaron added. "Is there any chance he might get out on bail between now and the trial?"

Sheriff Johnson answered, "I believe bail has been set at one million dollars. So no, he's not getting out."

"That's a relief," Aaron said. He didn't have to say it, but everyone in the room was thinking the same thing. Everyone feared that if Mark Becker did somehow make bail, he would change his mind once again and come after the rest of the family.

While Aaron and Todd peppered the investigators with questions, Jan sat back and listened. Hearing how her husband died was nearly as hard emotionally as coming to grips with the fact that he had been taken from her. Ellie reached over and put her arm around Jan. Even so, Jan felt very alone without Ed there beside her.

The briefing went on for another half hour. The family had more questions about how the investigation would proceed, when the case would go to trial, and what the state needed from them as it built its case. It was the first of what would prove to be many such briefings over the next several months. Of them all, this was the worst.

✦ ✦ ✦

After the briefing, the family returned to Jan's house. A few minutes later, Aaron said, "I'll be back. I need to take a walk."

"Do you want me to go with you?" Ellie asked.

"No," Aaron said. The rage he had felt as he sat and listened to the details of what Mark Becker did to his father boiled inside of him. He fought to keep it in check. "No, I uh … I just need to be by myself for a little while. I won't be gone long."

He took off walking, to where he didn't know. The image of Mark Becker standing over his father, stomping on him and cursing him, played over and over in his mind. *How could he do that to my father! All Dad ever did to him was encourage him and believe in him and do everything he could possibly do to try to help him make some right choices for once in his life, and this is how Mark repays him! Give me five minutes alone with him, and I'll repay him …* Aaron shook his head, trying to push those thoughts away. *Oh, God, what am I thinking? You said in Romans 12:19, "It is mine to avenge; I will repay." I have to leave this in your hands, God,* he prayed.

But you know what the worst part of this is? You know what nearly makes me crazy? If Becker turned his life around right now, if he asked the Lord to forgive him and save him and then ended up going to heaven, my dad would be the first in line to welcome him home. And if I know my father, he's probably talking to Jesus right now about Mark Becker. He's probably asking the Lord to give him another chance to choose to do what's right, because the Lord knows my father gave the kid enough second chances.

Aaron kept walking. He passed people and houses without noticing either. No one bothered him. No one stopped to ask him how he was doing. He just walked and walked and walked.

I know what Dad would say. He would tell me not to feel sorry for him, that he's in heaven right now because of what Jesus did when he died on a cross. Dad spent his entire life preparing for his final moment, and now that it is here, what am I supposed to say? — "No, Dad, you can't go?" Aaron walked along, turning that thought over and over in his mind. *I can't say that. But did it have to be like this?*

"Adversity is the test of character," Dad always said. He told his team over and over after the tornado that when bad things happen, it gives you an opportunity to show the character that is really

inside of you. So what is really *inside of you, Aaron Thomas? Are you going to get up and move forward, or are you going to let Mark Becker knock you down and out? What's it going to be?*

Oh, God, I can't do this on my own, he prayed.

Aaron turned and started back toward his mother's house. *If I can't live out right now all the lessons my dad taught me for my entire life, then his legacy won't mean much. "When the wind starts blowing, don't tell me about the hurricane; just bring the ship home,"* he used to say. *If he were here right now, Dad wouldn't want to hear all my excuses for how unfair it is that someone took him from me. He would just look me in the eye and say, "You know what you need to do, Aaron. Now do it. Do the right thing."* Aaron let out a long sigh. *I can do all things through Christ who gives me strength* — even this.*

Todd was not able to carve out time to be alone until later that evening. Candice could tell he needed a great deal of space, so she found an excuse to leave him at her parents' house all by himself. Like his brother, Todd seethed with anger after hearing the details of the murder. *Why did he have to kick Dad after he was down?* Even though he knew his father did not feel anything after the first shot, the very thought that this kid would kick his dad after he was on the ground, defenseless, infuriated Todd. Yet, even as he thought about that final act of cruelty, he couldn't help but think about the way his dad lived his life. *He dedicated himself to God's plan for his life, no matter what the cost — even if it meant his own life. And in the end it did.*

His mind raced back to endless conversations with his father. It wasn't about football. It was never about football. His father always said he wanted his legacy to be that he wasn't just a football coach but a man who tried to live a Christian life and impact others. A peace came over Todd. *Boy, did he ever do that. Dad reached the last kid God had for him to reach, and then he got to*

---

*Philippians 4:13.

*go home. I know, I know, the moment he walked into heaven, he heard the Father say, "Well done, my good and faithful servant."** That thought put a smile on Todd's face. That's all his dad ever wanted—to finish the work God had for him, and to do it the very best he could.

Todd let out a long sigh. *Oh, God, I miss him.* He sat down and began to weep. A deep ache came over him. Evil had come after his dad, but that didn't mean that evil had to win. For Todd, it could not win. *Oh, God, use my dad's death. Turn this evil into good,* he prayed.

Thoughts of how blessed Aaron's sons were to have known their grandfather swept through Todd's mind. He had always taken it for granted that his kids would as well. He had always assumed that if he and Candice had sons, they would someday play football for his dad and learn all the lessons from him that he had learned. His sorrow deepened as he realized it was all up to him now. It was up to him to pass on his dad's legacy to his own children. Todd sat still, alone, for a very long time. One thought came over him, one thought that gave him the strength to place Mark Becker in God's hands and leave his fate up to him: *One day, God is going to call me home. And I can see it. I can see Dad coming up to me with a hug and a grin that only my dad can give. And I can already hear him telling me, "Welcome home, pal!"*

After a long time, he stood up and said, "OK. I can do this."

---

*Matthew 25:21; Luke 19:17.

CHAPTER 20

GOOD-BYE

There are three things necessary to be successful in life:
faith and a relationship with God,
using our power to choose to do what is right,
and hard work.
ED THOMAS

OF ALL THE THINGS THE THOMAS FAMILY HAD TO DO IN THE
aftermath of the shooting, planning Ed's funeral was the easiest.
They really didn't have to plan anything. Ed already had everything
laid out for them. It wasn't that he expected to die anytime soon.
Not at all. It's just that Ed was the kind of man who had referees
lined up for football games five years in the future. So it didn't
surprise anyone that he had notes stuffed into his Bible listing all
the songs he wanted sung at his funeral service, along with a list of
pallbearers and Scriptures that should be read. Although Ed did not
leave a list of names of approved speakers, the family knew which
person he would have chosen. Al Kerns had worked with Ed longer
than anyone else, which made him a natural choice to lead things
off. Ed would also want his pastor, Brad Zinnecker, to speak. And
one of Ed's former players and a current coach, Kelly Williamson,
seemed like the perfect person to close out the service.

No, planning the service was not hard, especially since the
family knew where Ed wanted the focus. More than anything, he

wanted those in attendance and those who watched on television to hear the good news of how God sent his Son to die on the cross to pay the penalty for our sins, and how he rose again on the third day that we might have eternal life. Not only that, Ed wanted people to understand exactly how they could receive God's gift of eternal life by turning from their sins and placing their faith in Jesus alone. If Ed had walked into the room while the family was planning the service, that's where everything would have stopped. He wouldn't have wanted people to keep going on about him.

But that decision was not up to Ed, even though he had outlined most of the service ahead of time. The family wanted to share the gospel, but they also wanted to celebrate Ed's life and the impact he made on so many lives. The way the family saw it, the funeral wasn't an end, but the end of the beginning of the impact of the life of Ed Thomas. After the tornado, Ed spoke of rebuilding the town and making it stronger and better than it had ever been before. If he could, they knew he would get up and say the same thing now. The message of the funeral had to be: If Ed Thomas has impacted your life, go and do the same thing for someone else. Carry on his legacy, because that is what his entire life was all about.

The only hard part in planning Ed's funeral was figuring out how to fit into the church everyone who wanted to attend. The auditorium of First Congregational Church has a capacity of three hundred. No one knew how many people might show up on that day.

Sunday afternoon, the day before the funeral and four days after the shooting, they had their answer. The family scheduled a visitation time at which friends and family could come to the church to pay their respects to Ed and express their condolences to the family. They planned to start at 3:00 p.m. and end at 8:00. Once the crowd started lining up, the plans had to change. At one point, the line to get into the church stretched six blocks down the street from the church. Some people waited as long as four and a half hours to get inside. Police estimated that over five thousand people came through the line by the time the visitation finally ended at 11:30 p.m. Jan, Aaron, and Todd spoke to every single person who came through the line. They hardly even took a break.

However, before the doors opened to the public, Jan arranged for Dave and Joan Becker to come to the church to say their good-byes to Ed alone. While some people found this gesture hard to believe in light of the circumstances, for Jan and her sons, they never gave it a second thought. Of course, they would invite the Beckers to come to pay their respects to Ed. After all, Dave Becker had been the senior captain of Ed's first team in Parkersburg. The two of them served as deacons together at church, and the Beckers had been in Ed's Sunday school class for nearly thirty years. In the aftermath of the tornado, Dave and his youngest son, Scott, had spent many hours cleaning up the field and doing anything else Coach asked them to do.

Yet, there was more to the Thomases' decision than family connections. Jan put herself in Dave and Joan's shoes and looked at this tragedy from their perspective. She thought of all of the hopes and all of the dreams the Beckers had for their son—dreams now gone forever. As a parent herself, Jan tried to imagine what it would be like to carry the pain and the guilt Joan and Dave must surely feel. That is why Jan and the entire Thomas family were able to separate the family from this act. Mark Becker, not his parents or his brothers, committed this act. By reaching out to Dave and Joan, the Thomas family also sent a message to the entire community to do the same. If Jan, Aaron, and Todd reacted with anger and bitterness, the rest of the community may well follow suit. Instead, the Thomases made a choice to do the right thing, just as Ed would have done.

Dave and Joan arrived at 1:45 p.m. Shortly after 2:00, a funeral home official came over and said, "The extended family is here. We need to move this along to give them their time."

Jan responded, "Give the Beckers all the time they need."

✦ ✦ ✦

The morning of the funeral, Aaron got up early and went for a run. Running gave him time to think and to recharge himself for what he knew would be one of the hardest days of his life. A couple of days earlier, he had gone for a run like this when he sensed something he had never really sensed before. He felt God speaking to him, telling him that he needed to speak at the funeral. At first he tried to shove this aside, but he couldn't. Finally, he told the Lord, *All right. I'll speak. Next Sunday I'll ask Pastor to let me have a couple of minutes in the service.*

On his run on the morning of the funeral, Aaron sensed that same feeling again. Once again, God spoke, telling Aaron that he needed to speak. *OK, God. I will. Next Sunday. In front of the entire church. I'll do it.* Even as he prayed this, he knew deep down that this feeling had nothing to do with the following Sunday.

He ran harder and tried to clear his head. He ran down by the cemetery. His father's grave site was ready. The hole had been dug, and the tent over the site was in place. From the cemetery he turned and ran over toward the church. The police had put up barricades, making the street in front of the church one way to help the flow of traffic. They had also roped off the front of the church to keep the press from coming onto the church grounds. A designated media area was set up directly across the street. Camera crews from CNN, ESPN, and all the local television stations would soon fill the space.

Aaron continued running. As he ran past the church, he glanced at his watch. 8:00 a.m. The funeral was still two and a half hours away, yet people had already started lining up for one of the "first come, first served" closed-circuit-television seats in the church.

✦ ✦ ✦

Ed may have written out much of what he wanted in his funeral ahead of time, but the service deviated from his script in one important way: it lasted far longer than he would have ever wanted. While

Ed wouldn't have cared for the length, no one in attendance seemed to mind. No one was in a hurry to say good-bye.

Al Kerns set the tone of the morning when he placed a toy lawn tractor on the podium as he began his portion of the service. "My goal the next few minutes is that we go beyond mourning a death to remembering how this man lived," he started off, "because therein is Ed's message to us all. And to say that I lost my best friend in this case seems selfish, because Ed was the best friend to so many people. I've never known anyone like that. Ed had a lot of talents, but friendship was his best. He never met a person he didn't like. Whenever he met someone new, he came away saying, 'He's a nice guy,' or 'She's a really good person.' That's because Ed only saw the best in others.

"There were a lot of things that made Ed unique, and one of those was his clairvoyance. No matter where he was, he could sense a weed taking hold in his football field. I'm one of the guys who always gave him a hard time about the time and the energy he put into that field, but you know, this tractor and that field are metaphors for the way he lived. He treated that field like he treated every one of us. There must be millions upon millions of blades of grass out on that field, but he gave each one love and encouragement on a daily basis. He worked to make the roots deep so that it could withstand all kinds of pressure, especially when people walk on it and impede its upward growth. When bad things appeared, such as weeds and fungus, he eliminated them by physically pulling them out or by applying three times the amount of chemicals recommended by the EPA.

"It's funny. I'm color-blind. Yet hardly a day went by without Ed pointing toward the field and saying to me, 'Doesn't it look green?' I would agree, 'Yes, it sure is green,' even though I couldn't see it. Ed could.

"As I think back on my thirty-plus years of working side by side with Ed, I don't think about all the games he won or all the awards or the praise he received, even though all of that was well deserved.

No, all I really know from being around him for so long is that he made people around him wish to be better than we are by looking at the way he lived.

"Thanks, Ed, for being an inspiration. We will move on, but we will never forget."

If Ed had been in charge of the funeral, the moment Al finished speaking, Ed would have stood up and said, "All right, that's enough of that." But the service did not end there. After another of Ed's favorite songs was played, Pastor Brad Zinnecker spoke of Ed's character and the way in which his faith and his family came before football. Kelly Williamson followed. The family had asked him to close the service. "We know where Coach is right now," Kelly said. "He is in the very presence of God. But he isn't there because of all the good things he did. No, Coach is there, and you can be as well, because he trusted in Jesus Christ alone to save him." Kelly then invited all those in attendance who did not have a relationship with Christ to invite him into their hearts.

That was supposed to be the end. As Pastor Zinnecker took his place behind the podium and thanked everyone for attending, Aaron leaned over and whispered something to his mother. She nodded her head. Just as Pastor Zinnecker was about to offer the final prayer, Aaron walked up to the front. No one had planned this ahead of time, least of all Ed in his instructions about his own funeral, and yet, given the legacy Ed left behind, this was the only way the service could end.

"Quickly, I thought there are some things that need to be said that some might find inappropriate if anybody else said them," Aaron began. For two days he had wrestled with God over speaking at his father's funeral. He knew he was supposed to, but he did not think he would be able to do it. Yet, sitting there, listening to each of the speakers, he knew what he had to do.

"You know, my dad was terrible when he would lose. I don't know how my mom dealt with him. But it was my mom who would get him going. By Sunday afternoon, when the staff got together to meet, he was over the loss and ready to go again. The players all knew that Monday was going to be terrible. But it was part of getting back up.

"We stuck with this loss longer than I know he would like. There is no way he would want this to drag out for five days. And there is no way he would have waited four hours in line for anybody.

"But I'm going to tell you this and challenge you with this: You can be sad for the rest of the day, but come tomorrow, it's time to get going. That's the only way my dad's memory is going to live on. There is not one of us who can make up for what my dad did. There is not one of us here who will be Ed Thomas, but this can be a better place than it was with Ed Thomas. But for that to happen, it has got to come from each one of you.

"I don't care what your job is. If there was one thing I learned from my dad, it is that no job is too small. So I don't care what you do. When you step out tomorrow, you give it everything you've got. If work starts at 8:00 a.m., you make sure you're there at 7:57. You're not rolling in late. If you're done at 4:00 p.m., you work until 4:05. Don't shortchange anyone. Don't shortchange yourself.

"My father talked a lot about character. Character is you doing what is right when no one is looking and no one will know. My dad was a great man of character, and that's something I've taken from him. But come tomorrow, it's time we all get going.

"My father would be so proud to see this church full. Not because of these circumstances, but because of the fact that Kelly shared the message of how you can be saved and know where you're going. I know there are people in here who have never heard the gospel. I don't think that's the ultimate reason for my dad's death, but it will play a part.

"So as a community—and when I say community, it doesn't matter whether you are from Parkersburg, A-P, the state of Iowa, or anywhere else—if you truly honor and care about my father, come tomorrow, you will pick yourself up, get going, and do what you're supposed to do. If you want to honor my family and my father, it won't be just this week. The question is: Can you sustain it? He did it for thirty-three years here. Can you sustain it day in and day out, doing what's right, making people better, and taking care of each other? If you can do that, my father will live for a really long time through all of us. If you can't, that's when my father's death becomes a tragedy, and that's when it's a shame.

"Today, we can be sad. Come tomorrow, it's time we all get going. The true test of character is: How do we respond to adversity? This is adversity. How are you going to respond? What are you going to do tomorrow? God bless you all, and we thank you so much for coming and loving our father."

Aaron finished his remarks and took his seat next to his mother. By the time he finished speaking, it was clear to everyone in the room and to all those who watched on television that although Ed Thomas had passed, he had found a way to speak at his own funeral. His legacy and influence had only begun to build.*

After the service was over, the funeral procession made one last trip to the place that will always be synonymous with Ed's life and work: the Sacred Acre. The hearse drove slowly past the field where Ed had invested his life in the lives of his players and students. From there, the procession drove to the cemetery. All along the way, players from teams that A-P had competed against through the years lined up along both sides of the road, holding four fingers high, something Ed's teams did at the start of the fourth quarter of every game. For Ed, the four fingers held high said, "We will finish stronger than we started."

"Dad would have loved this," Aaron said to his mother. It was a fitting final tribute to a man who lived with heart and with great enthusiasm for four full quarters.

---

*For video of reactions to Coach Thomas's funeral, including the procession through the streets of Parkersburg, go to *www.youtube.com/watch?v=uYPQ84ONBdo*.

GETTING UP, MOVING FORWARD

Mark Becker was formally charged with first-degree murder the day after Ed Thomas's funeral. One week later, he entered a plea of not guilty by reason of insanity. The Thomas family learned later that Becker had been diagnosed as paranoid schizophrenic long before the shooting. He claimed voices in his head told him to shoot Coach Thomas because Coach was becoming "a devil tyrant." Prosecutors admitted that Becker was mentally ill but maintained that his actions on the day of the shooting demonstrated a full understanding of the difference between right and wrong.

The actual trial did not begin until the following February. The Thomas family attended every part of the trial, including the preliminary hearings. The jury deliberated for twenty-five hours before returning a guilty verdict. Becker was sentenced to life in prison without the possibility of parole. His court-appointed attorney immediately filed an appeal.

After the verdict was handed down, Todd Thomas told the press, "Our family is extremely relieved that a guilty verdict did come out. We do feel that justice has been served. And we feel like the system worked. Without a doubt, no verdict is ever going to replace Dad, but we do take comfort in knowing that he is in a better place. That allows us to keep moving forward."

Aaron Thomas added, "Our family is not over anything. The

Becker family is not over anything. We are still going to deal with this daily for as long as we live. Nothing that is going to happen, like Todd said, is going to bring my dad back. And now all we can do is for each of us to try to live the way he lived and by the example he set for all of us."

Part of the challenge both brothers face as they live out their father's legacy is the pain of his loss and the anger it stirs up within them. Aaron explained, "The real challenge verse for me has been Mark 11:25. 'And when you stand praying, if you hold anything against anyone, forgive him, so that your Father in heaven may forgive you your sins.' I read this verse right after the shooting, but I didn't want to hear it then. However, the Lord keeps bringing me back to it. Forgiveness is a daily decision I have to make. Do I still feel anger when I think about what happened? Sure. I probably always will. But I know I have to turn that over to God."

Todd answered the same question. "I never once questioned why my dad was taken from me that day. I am fully convinced that my dad had touched the last kid he was supposed to touch that day. There is no doubt that we are in a spiritual battle on this earth. Evil came after my dad that day, but evil did *not* win. The day of the funeral, many lives were changed. People saw a man who had finished strong, and peoples' lives were changed. Kelly Williamson said it best that day when he said, 'You know that you know that you know.' Our lives are nothing but a vapor on this earth. Without a doubt, my dad knew where he was going to live in eternity. And at eight o'clock that morning, Dad was doing what he does every day; and in an instant, he was standing before God. There is no doubt in my mind that he heard the words that we all long to hear: 'Well done, good and faithful servant!' "*

Shortly before the start of Mark Becker's trial, the Iowa state legislature began debate on what was called "The Ed Thomas Bill." The original version of the bill created an administrative process

---

*Matthew 25:21.

for hospitals to notify law enforcement personnel when releasing someone who had been receiving treatment for mental health issues and is subject to arrest by warrant or against whom charges are pending. However, the bill was essentially no different from existing Iowa statutes in place at the time of Coach Thomas's murder. If that bill had been law when Mark Becker was taken into custody on the Saturday before the shooting, he still would have been released without police notification.

Chris Luhring stayed in constant contact with legislators during the debate on this bill. At his urging, the Thomas family publicly stated that they did not support the proposed bill and asked that Ed Thomas's name be removed from it. Their actions prompted major changes in the proposed legislation. The new bill eliminated the requirement that law enforcement obtain a court order to hold a subject in a mental health facility for forty-eight hours. It also created a uniform process and form by which law enforcement may request to be notified of the discharge of someone taken to the hospital for serious mental impairment or of a person incapacitated by a chemical substance. Law enforcement must retrieve the individual within six hours of notification of the patient's release. Hospitals cannot hold the patient beyond the forty-eight hours already dictated by Iowa law. If hospitals fail to notify the proper authorities when requested, they face a civil penalty of $1,000 for the first offense, and $2,000 for each subsequent offense. The law also provides civil and criminal protections for those who comply with the law.

During debate on the strengthened bill, Aaron appeared before the subcommittee and urged the committee to honor his father by "doing the right thing." The state attorney general's office and the Department of Public Safety also went on record to state that the strengthened bill did not violate patient privacy rules dictated by HIPAA.

Even so, it appeared the bill might die in committee. On the final day of debate, Jan went to Des Moines and met with legislators, asking them to support the bill. Jan's visit turned the tide. The bill passed out of committee by unanimous vote. The Iowa House of Representatives then passed the bill by a vote of 90 to 0. The Senate followed suit with a 50 to 0 vote.

Governor Chet Culver signed the Ed Thomas Bill into law on March 24, 2010, with Jan, Aaron, and Todd in attendance. Aaron said on the occasion, "I think this is a bill my dad would be very proud of. This is a great thing, but obviously we wish we didn't have to have this bill in my dad's name."

✦ ✦ ✦

A few days after his father's funeral, the A-P school board asked Aaron to move back to Parkersburg as the school's athletic director. With the new school year just around the corner, he had to make a decision quickly. After much prayer and consideration, he resigned his position at Union High School in La Porte City, Iowa, and took over for his father at A-P. After selling their house in La Porte, Aaron and Ellie and their three sons moved in with Jan while their new house was being built in Parkersburg. Even one year after the tornado, there were no houses available to rent.

Taking over as A-P's athletic director fills every one of Aaron's days with reminders of his father. No one at the school calls him Coach Thomas, or even Mr. Thomas. Those titles will always belong to his father. For most people at the school, Aaron is simply Aaron. His players call him Coach.

In the summer of 2010, Aaron hired Alex Pollock as A-P's first new head football coach since 1975. Alex played for Ed from 1998 to 2001, including during the state championship season in 2001. The 2010 team went through the season undefeated before losing to Dike-New Hartford in the second round of the state playoffs. They finished the year with a 10 and 1 record, the same record as in Ed's final season.

✦ ✦ ✦

Todd and Candice had always planned on moving to Parkersburg. After his father's death, Todd felt a greater sense of urgency to be closer to his mother. Near the Parkersburg golf course, they built the home they had planned on building even before the tornado came. Shortly after Mark Becker's trial, Candice gave birth to their first child: a son. Todd also rejoined the A-P Falcon football coaching staff. Like his father, he now coaches the offensive linemen.

♦ ♦ ♦

In the weeks and months after Ed's death, Jan found herself turning to the book of Job over and over again. One phrase from early in the book leaped off the page to her. After Job suffered the deaths of his ten children, along with experiencing complete financial ruin followed by debilitating illness, his wife told him he should just curse God and die and get it over with. He responded to her, "Should we accept only good things from the hand of God and never anything bad?"* Jan could not get those words out of her mind as she wrestled with coming to grips with the loss she had suffered. She had read them before, but they never had the power they now had. As she turned them over and over in her mind, she came to the realization that if only good things happen in this world, no one would ever see a need for God. It is not that God causes sin. James 1:13 makes that crystal clear. Sin is, Jan came to realize, the absence of God. In a world filled with sin, bad things will inevitably happen. Acts of cruelty, such as the one that took her husband away, do not take God by surprise. He knew what would take place in the weight room that morning. However, in the midst of her pain, she knew that God was right there beside her. He made a promise in Hebrews 13:5–6 to which she was now clinging:

> "Never will I leave you;
> never will I forsake you."

---

*Job 2:10 NLT.

So we say with confidence,

"The Lord is my helper; I will not be afraid.
    What can mere mortals do to me?"

Even so, Jan found sleep elusive. Long before the shooting, she had started on a "Read through the Bible in a Year" calendar. She did most of her Bible reading during her restless hours late at night, which she followed with times of prayer. The two were her lifelines. Through it all, she found great comfort in knowing that Ed was rejoicing in the presence of God in heaven. That knowledge gave her the strength to face another day. However, it didn't make her miss him any less.

Later in the summer of 2009, Jan received a letter from one of the students who had witnessed the shooting in the weight room. The girl told Jan how she had struggled since the shooting, but also how the experience had caused her to reevaluate her own life. As a result, she gave her life to Jesus Christ and now felt confident that she would go to heaven someday. Reading the letter, Jan knew what Ed would say. He would say that if this girl were the only one to come to Christ as a result of his death, then it was all worth it. *But I know she won't be the only one!* The thought put a smile on Jan's face. She knew Ed had to be rejoicing in heaven as well.

In response, Jan wrote the girl:

I am so happy for your definite decision for Christ. This shooting is something that those of us who went through it will never truly get over. Don't let anybody tell you that you should be over it by now. Unless they have gone through something like this, they don't understand what it is like. I know how hard it had to be for you to witness this. I pray that someday you will know exactly why you were there. But for now, we have to trust God that he knew what he was doing by allowing you to be in there. He has a purpose for you, just as he has a purpose in this tragedy.

On the day after Ed's murder, Jan had prayed that God would use this act of evil to accomplish something good. This letter, and the many others that followed it, gave her a glimpse of how God was doing just that.

TEAM ROSTERS

Even with all the success Ed had on the field, his players always meant more to him than wins and losses. Therefore, it only seems appropriate to include the rosters of each of the teams he coached.

Northeast Hamilton Trojans

1972–74: Dennis Ackerman (manager), Denny Barnes, Scott Barrick, Ross Boyer, Jeff Brinkema, Randy Christianson, Randy Claussen, Murray Coleman, Monte Coleman, Ed Crawford, David Evans, Richard Evans, Robert Evans, Ron Evans, Eric Fonken, Max Fonken, Randy Greenfield, John Hall, Pat Hamilton, John Hempken, Curt Hensley, Doug Hill, Keith Holleland, Ed Holt, John Hoversten, Tim Keane, Kent Kennedy, Jerry Klaver, Lenny Klaver, Randy Klaver, Richard Klein, John Koop, Keith Leeds, Lloyd Luppes, Bruce Mark, Bruce Mechaelsen, Mike Menard, Tony Neubauer, Dallas Nibe, Jerry Ose, Randy Philbrook, Marlin Pruisman, Mike Pruisman, Tom Scott, Mike Sesker, Keith Smith, Glen Sorensen, Jeff Stotser, Denny Sweet, Rob Swenson, Harley Tapper, LaVerne Trueblood, Bob Ulrich, Phil Voge, Terry Wagoner, John Willems, Jon Williams, Kurt Williams, Mike Williams, Tony Woodall.

Parkersburg Crusaders

1975: Clint Allen, Ken Anderson, Dale Barrett, Don Barrett, Dave Becker, Jeff Becker, Bill Blum, Randy Brocka, Jeff Church, Stan

Claassen, Gary Collings, Ken Eggers, Doug Hogelucht, Kent Hoppenworth, Lu Jansen, Terry Johnson, Denton Kannegieter, Paul Klingenborg, Sam Klinkenborg, Doug Krull, Bryan LaVelle, Dave LaVelle, Jim McClatchey, Dave Mehmen, Greg Melcher, Lew Rieken, Tony Scheidecker, Walt Scheidecker, Kurt Walters, Mark Wix, Dan Wygle, Tim Wygle.

1976: Clint Allen, Dana Anderson, Ken Anderson, Lindsey Bakker, Don Barrett, Jeff Becker, Rick Berends, Kevin Buchanan, Stan Claassen, Gary Collings, Larry Cornelius, Ken Eggers, Jeff Glaw, Kevin Graves, Kent Hoppenworth, Lu Jansen, Terry Johnson, Brent Kannegieter, Sam Klinkenborg, Doug Krull, Cary Lambros, Bryan LaVelle, Randy Luhring, Greg Melcher, Bucky Nitcher, Greg Prohaska, Brad Rasmussen, Mike Rule, Tony Scheidecker, Walt Scheidecker, Bryan Schipper, Todd Schneiderman, Gary Schwarz, Steve Spain, Daryl Uhlenhopp, Mark Wix, Dan Wygle, Tim Wygle, Tony Wygle.

1977: Greg Allspach, Dana Anderson, Brian Bakker, Jeff Becker, Rick Berends, Kevin Buchanan, Brian Buss, Mike Buss, Brent Card, Brian Card, Jerry Claassen, Gary Collings, Larry Cornelius, Ron Eilderts, Jeff Glaw, Kevin Graves, Dave Hogelucht, Kent Hoppenworth, Brad Humphrey, Ron Jansen, Brent Kannegieter, Sam Klinkenborg, Cary Lambros, Randy Luhring, Mike Meeker, Greg Melcher, Bucky Nitcher, Tony Patterson, Greg Prohaska, Mike Rule, Tony Scheidecker, Walt Scheidecker, Bryan Schipper, Todd Schneiderman, James Siems, Jon Siems, Steve Spain, Scott Thorne, Daryl Uhlenhopp, Gregg Vanderholt, Larry Van Dyke, Matt Wagoner, Kurt Walters, Scott Wildeboer, Mark Wix, Tim Wygle, Tony Wygle.

1978: Greg Allspach, Dana Anderson, Kelly Anderson, Brian Bakker, Kevin Buchanan, Brian Buss, Mike Buss, Brent Card, Brian Card, Don Cashatt, Gary Collings, Mike DeGroote, Ron

Eilderts, Jeff Glaw, Todd Glaw, Kevin Graves, Mark Graves, Brian Hackman, Dave Hogelucht, Kreg Hoppenworth, Brad Humphrey, Ron Jansen, Mitch Johnson, Brent Kannegieter, Dean Lindeman, Randy Luhring, Mike Meeker, Greg Melcher, Jeff Melcher, Tony Patterson, Mike Paup, Greg Prohaska, Mike Rule, Tony Scheidecker, Todd Schneiderman, Keith Schrage, Gregg Vanderholt, Larry Van Dyke, Dave Walitshek, Kurt Walters, Scott Wildeboer, Todd Wildeboer, Mark Wix, Tim Wygle, Tony Wygle.

1979: Greg Allspach, Kelly Anderson, Cary Bergman, Brian Buss, Mike Buss, Brent Card, Brian Card, Rick Cashatt, Kevin Dann, Mike DeGroote, Ron Eilderts, Dean Everts, Dan Gerdes, Jeff Glaw, Todd Glaw, Kevin Graves, Mark Graves, Irv Haan, Brian Hackman, Dave Hogelucht, Kreg Hoppenworth, Ron Jansen, Scott Johnson, Dean Lindeman, Randy Luhring, Bruce Mattingly, Brett Meeker, Mike Meeker, Jeff Melcher, Tony Patterson, Dave Paup, Mike Paup, Greg Prohaska, Mike Rule, Todd Schneiderman, Keith Schrage, Rex Tomkins, Grant Vanderholt, Gregg Vanderholt, Larry Van Dyke, Dave Walitshek, Todd Wildeboer.

1980: Greg Allspach, Brian Anderson, Kelly Anderson, Brian Buss, Mike Buss, Brent Card, Brian Card, Rick Cashatt, Kevin Dann, Jack Denholm, Ron Eilderts, Dean Everts, Todd Glaw, Mark Graves, Irv Haan, Dave Hogelucht, Kreg Hoppenworth, Ron Jansen, Mike Johnson, Scott Johnson, Jerry Kneppe, Dean Lindeman, Bruce Mattingly, Brett Meeker, Mike Meeker, Jeff Melcher, Greg Monroe, Tony Patterson, Dave Paup, Mike Paup, Tracy Rasmussen, Pat Rule, Keith Schrage, Jeff Simkins, Dale Stickley, Brett Thorne, Grant Vanderholt, Larry Van Dyke, Danny Walitshek, Dave Walitshek, Todd Wildeboer.

1981: Rick Adelmund, Brian Anderson, Kelly Anderson, Daran Bartels, Tracy Brouwer, Scott Buchanan, Rick Cashatt, Tim

Cuvelier, Kevin Dann, Terry DeGroote, Jack Denholm, Dean Everts, Greg Glaw, Todd Glaw, Irv Haan, Kurt Hempen, Mike Johnson, Scott Johnson, Kent Karsjens, Jeff Kessler, Dean Lindeman, Bruce Mattingly, Brett Meeker, Dale Meester, Randy Myers, Merle Niehaus, Dave Paup, Mike Paup, Juha Raisanen, Rodney Reints, Pat Rule, Doug Schipper, Keith Schrage, Jeff Simkins, Brett Thorne, Rex Tomkins, Scott Tomkins, Larry Van Dyke, Kraig Vry, Danny Walitshek, Dave Walitshek, Donny Walitshek, Todd Wildeboer, Jeff Yost.

1982: Brian Anderson, Daran Bartels, Jeff Bosley, Tracy Brouwer, Scott Buchanan, Dave Cleary, Darren Coy, Tim Cuvelier, Kevin Dann, Dan DeGroot, Terry DeGroote, Jack Denholm, Dean Everts, Irv Haan, Kurt Hempen, Mike Johnson, Scott Johnson, Tim Johnson, Kent Karsjens, Jeff Kessler, Bobby Klinkenborg, Klint Knock, Kurt Luhring, Bruce Mattingly, Brett Meeker, Dale Meester, Randy Myers, Dave Paup, Rodney Reints, Pat Rule, Doug Schipper, Jeff Simkins, Shawn Smeins, Brent Sodders, Darin Stokes, Brett Thorne, Rex Tomkins, Galon (Buddy) Vanderholt, Danny Walitshek, Donny Walitshek, Mike Wise, Jeff Yost.

1983: Clint Ackerson, Jack Ackerson, Cory Allspach, Daran Bartels, Clint Bergman, Jeff Bosley, Tracy Brouwer, Tim Cashatt, Dave Cleary, Darren Coy, Tim Cuvelier, Mike Davis, Dan DeGroot, Terry DeGroote, Jack Denholm, Rusty Eddy, Brian Elliot, Dean Everts, Mike Good, Kurt Hempen, Mike Johnson, Kent Karsjens, Jeff Kessler, Bobby Klinkenborg, Klint Knock, Brad Knudson, Kurt Luhring, Vance Mennen, Todd Miller, Randy Myers, Pat Rule, Doug Schipper, John Simkins, Chad Smeins, Shawn Smeins, Darin Stokes, Brett Thorne, Scott Tomkins, Galon (Buddy) Vanderholt, Danny Walitshek, Donny Walitshek, Mike Wise, Jeff Yost.

1984: Clint Ackerson, Cory Allspach, Greg Asche, Daran Bartels,

Jeff Bosley, Tracy Brouwer, David Brundage, Scott Buchanan, Tim Cashatt, David Cleary, Brian Coy, Darren Coy, David Coy, Jason Coy, Tim Cuvelier, Dan DeGroot, Richard DeGroot, Terry DeGroote, Jack Denholm, Brian Elliot, Dean Everts, Kurt Hempen, Quint Jansen, Brian Kelly, Jeff Kessler, Bobby Klinkenborg, Klint Knock, Brad Knudson, Troy Kramer, Jerry Melcher, Todd Miller, Jerry Mitchell, Randy Myers, Glenn Patterson, Jeff Patterson, Darcy Rasmussen, Doug Schipper, John Simkins, Chad Smeins, Shawn Smeins, Darin Stokes, Galon (Buddy) Vanderholt, Kraig Vry, Donny Walitshek, Jerry Wessels, Mike Wise, Jeff Yost.

1985: Clint Ackerson, Cory Allspach, Greg Asche, Trent Bierstedt, Nick Bosley, Dan Bruns, Chad Buss, Tim Cashatt, David Cleary, Brian Coy, Craig Coy, Darren Coy, Doug DeGroot, Richard DeGroot, Jack Denholm, Bruce DeVries, Rusty Eddy, Dave Everts, Jim Graham, Quint Jansen, Jimmy Johnson, Martin Johnson, Billy Kelly, Bobby Klinkenborg, Klint Knock, Brad Knudson, Holger Lackhoff, Kurt Luhring, Jerry Melcher, Dean Miller, Todd Miller, Jerry Mitchell, Chad Nieuwsma, Glenn Patterson, Darcy Rasmussen, Eric Scheidecker, David Schneiderman, Tim Schnell, Shawn Schroeder, Shawn Seehusen, John Simkins, Chad Smeins, Shawn Smeins, Darin Stokes, Galon (Buddy) Vanderholt, Wade Wagoner, Paul Watters, Peter Watters, Jerry Wessels, Ken West, Jeff Wetzig, Mike Wetzig, Matt Wildeboer, Mike Wise.

1986: David Adamson, Cory Allspach, Greg Asche, Dan Bruns, Bobby Burton, Chad Buss, Tim Cashatt, Brian Coy, Craig Coy, Doug DeGroot, Jim Denholm, Rusty Eddy, Derek Etjen, Dave Everts, Jim Graham, Paul Hoogestraat, Neil Ihde, Quint Jansen, Jim Johnson, Jay Jordan, Brad Knudson, Jerry Melcher, Dean Miller, Matt Miller, Todd Miller, Jerry Mitchell, Mike Neavins, Chad Oldenburger, Glenn Patterson, Darcy Rasmussen, Eric

Scheidecker, David Schneiderman, Shawn Seehusen, John Simkins, Chad Smeins, Mike Timmer, Rod Truax, Charles Watters, Paul Watters, Peter Watters, Jerry Wessels, Ken West, Matt Wildeboer.

1987: David Adamson, Greg Asche, Dan Bruns, Bobby Burton, Chad Buss, Chad Campbell, Mitch Cashatt, Brian Coy, Craig Coy, Jason Coy, Jim Denholm, Ryan Eddy, Chad Eiklenborg, Jim Graham, Paul Hoogestraat, Pat Hosch, Neil Ihde, Quint Jansen, Jim Johnson, Mike Johnson, Wes Johnson, Jay Jordan, Jon Klinkenborg, Jerry Melcher, Matt Miller, Jerry Mitchell, Brian Myers, Mike Neavins, Chad Oldenburger, Glenn Patterson, Darcy Rasmussen, Dan Rule, Eric Scheidecker, David Schneiderman, Shawn Seehusen, Rod Truax, Charles Watters, Paul Watters, Peter Watters, Ken West, Matt Wildeboer, Chris Zubak.

1988: David Adamson, Scott Alberts, Neil Brungard, Dan Bruns, Bob Burton, Chad Buss, Jeremy Buss, Chad Campbell, Mitch Cashatt, Jason Coy, Ryan Eddy, Chad Eiklenborg, Derek Etjen, Blaine Hartman, Scott Hofer, Adam Hoogestraat, Paul Hoogestraat, John Jordan, Pat Hosch, John Huisman, Neil Ihde, Jim Johnson, Wes Johnson, Jay Jordan, Jon Klinkenborg, Mike Neavins, Derek Neymeyer, Cory Norris, Shane Oldenburger, Dan Rule, Eric Scheidecker, Scott Schipper, Nathan Schnell, Dirk Smeins, Nate Smith, Jason Stickley, Rod Truax, Rusty Truax, Charles Watters, Paul Watters, Peter Watters, Ken West, Casey Wiegmann, Matt Wildeboer, Chris Zubak.

1989: David Adamson, Scott Alberts, Neil Brungard, Bob Burton, Jeremy Buss, Chad Campbell, Sergio Cardenas, Mitch Cashatt, Darin Christians, Josh Clark, Ryan Eddy, Chad Eiklenborg, Jeremy Gosch, Scott Hofer, Paul Hoogestraat, Pat Hosch, John Huisman, Neil Ihde, Wes Johnson, Jay Jordan, Charlie Kellum,

Jon Klinkenborg, Jon Mansheim, Gregg Meester, Matt Miller, Brian Myers, Mike Neavins, Derek Neymeyer, Cory Norris, Shane Oldenburger, Dan Rule, Scott Schipper, Nathan Schnell, Rob Schuck, Dirk Smeins, Nate Smith, Jason Stickley, Rod Truax, Rusty Truax, Bret Wagoner, Casey Wiegmann, Chris Wygle, Chris Zubak.

1990: Scott Alberts, Jon Blevins, Neil Brungard, Jeremy Buss, Chad Campbell, Aaron Capron, Mitch Cashatt, Darin Christians, Josh Clark, Jason Coy, Ryan Eddy, Chad Eiklenborg, J.J. Hansel, Scott Hofer, Adam Hoogestraat, Pat Hosch, John Huisman, Matt Jansen, Wes Johnson, Zach Junker, Charlie Kellum, Jon Klinkenborg, Zach McLean, Gregg Meester, Brian Myers, Derek Neymeyer, Cory Norris, Shane Oldenburger, Dalen Schipper, Scott Schipper, Rob Schuck, Jason Simon, Dirk Smeins, Nate Smith, Jason Stickley, Jed Thompson, Casey Wiegmann, Chris Wygle, Trevor Youngberg, Chris Zubak.

1991: Chad Adelmund, Scott Alberts, Randy Berends, Jon Blevins, Neil Brungard, Jeremy Buss, Mark Campbell, Aaron Capron, Darin Christians, Josh Clark, Clint Dickes, Deren Etjen, Nate Everts, Chris Fleshner, Ryan Fleshner, Scott Hofer, Adam Hoogestraat, Joel Hoogestraat, John Huisman, Matt Jacobson, Matt Jansen, John Jordan, Zach Junker, Lee Klinkenborg, Calley Kruger, Aaron Maitland, Zach McLean, Brad Meester, Gregg Meester, Jamie Miller, Derek Neymeyer, Cory Norris, Shane Oldenburger, Bud Rewerts, Dalen Schipper, Scott Schipper, Steve Schipper, Clay Schrage, Rob Schuck, Chad Shepard, Jason Simon, John Simon, Dirk Smeins, Ty Smeins, Nate Smith, Jason Stickley, Jed Thompson, Josh Timmer, Cody Wiegmann, Kelly Williamson, Chris Wygle, Trevor Youngberg.

Aplington-Parkersburg Falcons

1992: Chad Adelmund, Trent Alberts, Randy Berends, Jon Blevins, Tim Blevins, Aaron Buss, Mark Campbell, Aaron Capron, Darin Christians, Ben Dao, Darian DeVries, Jared DeVries, Clint Dickes, Jade Dix, Clint Dohlman, Chad Druvenga, Deren Etjen, Cory Everts, Nate Everts, Chris Fleshner, Ryan Fleshner, Derek Harken, Joel Hoogestraat, Pete Hosch, Ben Huisinga, Matt Jacobson, Matt Jansen, Alex Johnson, Chadd Johnson, D.J. Johnson, Zach Junker, Josh Kerns, Tim Kolder, Cory Koop, Brett Kramer, Calley Kruger, T.J. Leonard, Nate Lester, Travis Lester, Jereme Lockwood, Aaron Maitland, Josh McClatchey, Matt McLean, Zach McLean, Brad Meester, Gregg Meester, Chet Mellema, Jamie Miller, Pat Miller, Christian Mohrmann, Jon Muller, Joe Neymeyer, Grant Ostercamp, Dalen Schipper, Steve Schipper, Travis Schipper, Clay Schrage, Rob Schuck, Brad Sessler, Chad Shepard, Chris Siems, Chris Simon, Jason Simon, John Simon, Ty Smeins, Joel Stahl, Greg Stockdale, Justin Stockdale, Jed Thompson, Josh Timmer, Cody Wiegmann, Kelly Williamson, Chris Wygle, Trevor Youngberg, Andy Zylstra.

1993: Trent Alberts, Scott Arends, Travis Baker, Randy Berends, Bryan Blair, Jon Blevins, Tim Blevins, Aaron Buss, Mark Campbell, Aaron Capron, Jared DeVries, Clint Dickes, Jade Dix, Seth Dohrn, Deren Etjen, Nate Everts, Ryan Fleshner, Rex Goodrich, Justin Hansel, Derek Harken, Joel Hoogestraat, Pete Hosch, Mark Hubbard, Ben Huisinga, Travis Ibeling, Matt Jacobson, Matt Jansen, Alex Johnson, Chadd Johnson, D.J. Johnson, Zach Junker, Nate Kannegieter, Josh Kerns, Tim Kolder, Brett Kramer, Dennis Kramer, Calley Kruger, Brandon Krusey, Nate Lester, Travis Lester, Jereme Lockwood, Chris Luck, Chris Luhring, Josh McClatchey, Matt McLean, Zach McLean, Brad Meester, Jeff Mennen, Jamie Miller, Pat Miller, Jarrod Mudderman, Jon Muller, Grant Ostercamp, Josh Peters, Dalen Schipper, Ryan Schipper, Steve Schipper, Gary Schnell, Clay Schrage, Chris Siems, Chris Simon, Jason Simon, John Simon, Ty Smeins, Joel Stahl, Greg Stockdale, Aaron Thomas, Jed Thompson, Josh Timmer, Justin Uhlenhopp, Landon Uhlenhopp, Cody Wiegmann, Kelly Williamson, Joe Wilmer, Jamie Woodley, Trevor Youngberg, Andy Zylstra.

1994: Trent Alberts, Scott Arends, Travis Baker, Randy Berends, Bryan Blair, Tim Blevins, Jason Brocka, Justin Buck, Aaron Buss, Mark Campbell, Ben Cutler, Rick DeGroote, Dusty DeVries, Clint Dickes, Jade Dix, Seth Dohrn, Nate Everts, Nick Everts, Ryan Fleshner, Rob Gorter, Chris Grandon, Derek Harken, Ivan Harken, Gregg Hinders, Joel Hoogestraat, Pete Hosch, Mark Hubbard, Ben Huisinga, Travis Ibeling, Matt Jacobson, Chadd Johnson, Ryan Junker, Aaron Kampman, Nate Kannegieter, Josh Kerns, Tim Kolder, Brett Kramer, Dennis Kramer, Jason Kramer, Klint Kramer, Calley Kruger, Brandon Krusey, Nate Lester, Travis Lester, Jereme Lockwood, Chris Luhring, Aaron Maitland, Josh McClatchey, Brad Meester, Jeff Mennen, Jamie Miller, Joey Miller, Pat Miller, Jarrod Mudderman, James Muller, Grant Ostercamp, Josh Peters, Jared Reints, Ryan Schipper, Steve Schipper, Gary Schnell, Andy Schrage, Clay Schrage, Brandon Sessler, Chris Siems, Chris Simon, John Simon, Ty Smeins, Joel Stahl, Chuck Stockdale, Greg Stockdale, Matt Stockdale, Aaron Thomas, Josh Timmer, Cory Troyna, Reggie Truax, Justin Uhlenhopp, Landon Uhlenhopp, Cody Wiegmann, Kelly Williamson, John Wilmer, Jamie Woodley.

1995: Trent Alberts, Bryan Blair, Dan Blevins, Tim Blevins, Justin Buck, Aaron Buss, Taylor Buss, Ben Cutler, Dusty DeVries, Derek Dietrich, Jade Dix, Seth Dohrn, Andy Everts, Chris Grandon, Derek Harken, Gregg Hinders, Travis Holfaster, Jeremiah Hook, Pete Hosch, Mark Hubbard, Ben Huisinga, Travis Ibeling, Cory Jensen, Chadd Johnson, Ryan Junker, Aaron Kampman,

Nate Kannegieter, Jake Kerns, Josh Kerns, Kirk Klooster, Brent Kolder, Brett Kramer, Jason Kramer, Brandon Krusey, Josh LaVelle, Nate Lester, Jereme Lockwood, Chris Luhring, Bryon Marks, Justin Mehmen, Jeff Mennen, Pat Miller, Jarrod Mudderman, James Muller, Grant Ostercamp, Josh Peters, Andy Pollock, Brandon Schipper, Danny Schipper, Ryan Schipper, Silas Schipper, Ryan Schrage, Scott Schrage, Chris Siems, Chuck Stockdale, Greg Stockdale, Matt Stockdale, Steve Temple, Aaron Thomas, Todd Thomas, Cory Troyna, Brandon Uhlenhopp, Justin Uhlenhopp, Landon Uhlenhopp, Trent Vanlengen, Carl VanSant, John Wilmer, Jamie Woodley, Brian Zylstra.

1996: Scott Ashby, Bryan Blair, Dan Blevins, Jesse Buck, Justin Buck, Taylor Buss, Ben Cutler, Brandon Cutler, Dusty DeVries, Derek Dietrich, Ross Dix, Seth Dohrn, Mike Graham, Chris Grandon, Gregg Hinders, Travis Holzfaster, Mark Hubbard, Cory Jensen, Ryan Junker, Jacob Kafka, Aaron Kampman, Nate Kannegieter, Jake Kerns, Kirk Klooster, Brent Kolder, Dennis Kramer, Jason Kramer, Brandon Krusey, Josh LaVelle, Chris Luhring, Jeremy Madsen, Justin Manifold, Bryon Marks, Neil Meester, Travis Meester, Justin Mehmen, Jeff Mennen, Dustin Mlenar, Bret Morris, Jarrod Mudderman, James Muller, Steve Nielsen, Brian Noble, Chris Patterson, Craig Peters, Josh Peters, Andy Pollock, Chris Sale, Ryan Schipper, Silas Schipper, Gary Schnell, Ryan Schrage, Scott Schrage, Ryan Siems, Brandon Smith, Chuck Stockdale, Matt Stockdale, J.T. Strang, Steve Temple, Aaron Thomas, Todd Thomas, Adam Tjeerdsma, Cory Troyna, Cody Ubben, Brandon Uhlenhopp, Justin Uhlenhopp, Landon Uhlenhopp, Luke Uhlenhopp, Trent Vanlengen, Carl VanSant, Kyle Weber, Joe Wilmer, John Wilmer, Jamie Woodley.

1997: Brad Arends, Bryan Blair, Carl Brouwer, Jesse Buck, Justin Buck, Taylor Buss, Ben Cutler, Brandon Cutler, Dusty DeVries, Derek Dietrich, Anthony Dix, Ross Dix, Zach Eggers, Chris

Grandon, Kyle Grandon, Ashley Graves, Trent Hackman, Gregg Hinders, Klay Hoppenworth, Paul Hubbard, Jon Jacobson, Ryan Junker, Jacob Kafka, Aaron Kampman, James Kennedy, Jake Kerns, Kirk Klooster, Brent Kolder, Jason Kramer, Mitch Kurtz, Josh LaVelle, Nick Lovrien, Brian Madsen, Jeremy Madsen, Justin Mehmen, Zach Meyer, Jonny Miller, Dustin Mlenar, James Muller, Steve Nielsen, Chris Patterson, Craig Peters, Andy Pollock, Jeff Ridder, Silas Schipper, Gary Schnell, Landon Schrage, Ryan Schrage, Scott Schrage, Aaron Simon, Matt Stockdale, J.T. Strang, Josh Strang, Steve Temple, Todd Thomas, Luke Thompson, Adam Tjeerdsma, Brett Tjeerdsma, Cory Troyna, Cody Ubben, Brandon Uhlenhopp, Trent Vanlengen, Kyle Weber, Kurt Wessels, John Wilmer.

1998: Brad Becker, Dan Blevins, Carl Brouwer, Jesse Buck, Taylor Buss, Brandon Cutler, Jay DeVries, Derek Dietrich, Anthony Dix, Ross Dix, Kyle Grandon, Ashley Graves, Mark Harken, Klay Hoppenworth, Paul Hubbard, Dale Huisinga, Jon Jacobson, Arend Johnson, Nolan Junker, Jacob Kafka, James Kennedy, Jake Kerns, Luke Klahsen, Kirk Klooster, Thomas Kresse, Mitch Kurtz, Josh LaVelle, Jon Manifold, Joel Marks, Travis Meester, Justin Mehmen, Zach Meyer, Jonny Miller, Brett Mlenar, Dustin Mlenar, Brett Morris, Matt Morris, Steve Nielsen, Aaron Noble, Brian Noble, Chris Patterson, Wes Patterson, Craig Peters, Alex Pollock, Andy Pollock, Derrick Rogers, Dustin Schell, Mark Schipper, Silas Schipper, Landon Schrage, Ryan Schrage, Scott Schrage, Aaron Simon, Josh Strang, J.T. Strang, Steve Temple, Todd Thomas, Luke Thompson, Adam Tjeerdsma, Cody Ubben, Brandon Uhlenhopp, Trent Vanlengen, Kyle Weber, Dallas Wessels, Kurt Wessels.

1999: Nick Beebe, Carl Brouwer, Brandon Cutler, Brandon Cuvelier, Jay DeVries, Anthony Dix, Ross Dix, Nick Doyle, Joe Edwards, Joey Foster, Christian Goldammer, Faron Good, Chad

Grandon, Kyle Grandon, Jesse Hepler, Kade Hoppenworth, Klay Hoppenworth, Paul Hubbard, Dale Huisinga, Quentin Huisman, Jon Jacobson, Arend Johnson, Casey Jones, Jacob Kafka, Erik Kalkwarf, Curt Kampman, James Kennedy, Luke Klahsen, Kent Klooster, Nick Koenen, Mitch Kurtz, Joel Marks, Josh McConnell, Nate McCracken, Zach Meyer, Jonny Miller, Brett Mlenar, Dustin Mlenar, Brett Morris, Matt Morris, Steve Nielsen, Aaron Noble, Brian Noble, Chris Patterson, Wes Patterson, Craig Peters, Alex Pollock, Joel Reints, Kendrick Renken, Derrick Rogers, Dustin Schell, Mark Schipper, Landon Schrage, Taylor Schrage, Chris Sents, Aaron Simon, Josh Strang, J.T. Strang, Andrew Tenney, Luke Thompson, Brynn Thorne, Adam Tjeerdsma, Scott Tjeerdsma, Ryan Troyna, Cody Ubben, Nick Walters, Dallas Wessels, Kurt Wessels, Dustin Wygle.

2000: Zach Anderson, Mark Becker, Riley Brocka, Carl Brouwer, Shannon Cox, Jay DeVries, Anthony Dix, Casey Dix, Nick Doyle, Joe Edwards, Joe Eggers, Martin Ennor, Rich Fisher, Mark Freed, Chad Grandon, Matt Harken, Jay Harkless, Jesse Hepler, Kade Hoppenworth, Klay Hoppenworth, Paul Hubbard, Quentin Huisman, Jon Jacobson, Arend Johnson, Erik Kalkwarf, Mike Kalkwarf, Curt Kampman, Austin Kannegieter, Jake Klahsen, Luke Klahsen, Kent Klooster, Greg Koenen, Nick Koenen, Mitch Kurtz, Adam Limburg, Joel Marks, Keith McClatchey, Zach Meyer, Jonny Miller, Matt Morris, Aaron Noble, Wes Patterson, Alex Pollock, Grant Pollock, Joel Reints, Kendrick Renken, Derrick Rogers, Dustin Rogers, Clint Schipper, Mark Schipper, Ryan Schnell, Landon Schrage, Taylor Schrage, Aaron Simon, Kyle Simon, Cole Spree, Josh Strang, Luke Thompson, Brynn Thorne, Scott Tjeerdsma, Ryan Troyna, Nick Walters, Dallas Wessels, Kurt Wessels, Levi Whitmire, Caleb Wiegmann, Derrick Wygle, Dustin Wygle.

2001: Zach Anderson, Mark Becker, Riley Brocka, Zach Church,

Brandon Ciavarelli, Justin Cordes, Shannon Cox, Jay DeVries, Casey Dix, Nick Doyle, Joe Edwards, Joe Eggers, Rich Fisher, Jason Freeseman, Vince Gisch, Chad Grandon, Jordan Green, Matt Harken, Jay Harkless, Kyle Harms, Blake Harris, Kade Hoppenworth, Brandon Huisman, Quentin Huisman, Andy Jacobson, Randy Kafka, Erik Kalkwarf, Mike Kalkwarf, Curt Kampman, Austin Kannegieter, Jake Klahsen, Luke Klahsen, Kent Klooster, Greg Koenen, Nick Koenen, Casey Kyhl, Adam Limburg, Linus Lindh, Joel Marks, Keith McClatchey, Matt Morris, Enoch Ng, Aaron Noble, Mark Noble, Eric Ooms, Brandon Patterson, Wes Patterson, Alex Pollock, Grant Pollock, Joel Reints, Kendrick Renken, Derrick Rogers, Dustin Rogers, Clint Schipper, Mark Schipper, Brandon Schrage, Taylor Schrage, Kyle Simon, Cole Spree, David Thompson, Brynn Thorne, Scott Tjeerdsma, Ryan Troyna, Curtis Tyler, Nick Walters, Dallas Wessels, Levi Whitmire, Caleb Wiegmann, Derrick Wygle, Dustin Wygle.

2002: Adam Aalderks, Jon Abkes, Jacob Allspach, Zach Anderson, Mark Becker, Dave Bellows, Riley Brocka, Braden Claassen, Justin Cordes, Shannon Cox, Casey Dix, Nick Doyle, Joe Edwards, Joe Eggers, Kyle Everts, Rich Fisher, Jason Freeseman, Vince Gisch, Chad Grandon, Matt Harken, Jay Harkless, Kyle Harms, Blake Harris, Kade Hoppenworth, Andy Jacobson, Rick Johnson, Erik Kalkwarf, Mike Kalkwarf, Curt Kampman, Austin Kannegieter, Jake Klahsen, Kent Klooster, Greg Koenen, Nick Koenen, Tom Koenen, Casey Kyhl, Joey Larson, Adam Limburg, Keith McClatchey, Tyrus Meester, Caleb Meyer, Tyler Nevenhoven, Austin Niederhauser, Mark Noble, Schuylar Oordt, Brandon Patterson, Grant Pollock, Jordan Proctor, Joel Reints, Kendrick Renken, Dustin Rogers, Clint Schipper, Brandon Schrage, Taylor Schrage, Kyle Sharp, Kyle Simon, Kyle Spree, Nate Studnicka, Nick Tjeerdsma, Scott Tjeerdsma, Ryan Troyna, Curtis Tyler, Jesse Tyler, Clint Uhlnehopp, Nick Walters,

Jon Wangler, Levi Whitmire, Caleb Wiegmann, Nate Woodley, Derrick Wygle.

2003: Adam Aalderks, Jon Abkes, Jacob Allspach, Zach Anderson, Mark Becker, Dave Bellows, Riley Brocka, Evan Capper, Braden Claassen, Shannon Cox, Casey Dix, Ryan Downs, Joe Eggers, Jessie Farley, Rich Fisher, Jason Freeseman, Tommy Gisch, Vince Gisch, Colin Groeneveld, Matt Harken, Creed Harkless, Kyle Harms, Blake Harris, Andy Jacobson, Ethan Johnson, Rick Johnson, Craig Junker, Austin Kannegieter, Jake Klahsen, Greg Koenen, Justin Koenen, Tom Koenen, Joey Larson, Adam Limburg, Keith McClatchey, Will McCord, Bo Meester, Tyrus Meester, Caleb Meyer, Tyler Nevenhoven, Jesse Nitcher, Eric Ooms, Schuylar Oordt, Brandon Patterson, Justin Peters, Grant Pollock, Jordan Proctor, Nate Redman, Kyle Reisinger, Dustin Rogers, Clint Schipper, Michael Sharp, Kyle Simon, Kyle Slifer, Kyle Spree, Nate Studnicka, Michael Taylor, Nick Tjeerdsma, Curtis Tyler, Jesse Tyler, Clint Uhlnehopp, Levi Whitmire, Caleb Wiegmann, Nate Woodley, Derrick Wygle.

2004: Adam Aalderks, Jon Abkes, Matt Adelmund, Jacob Allspach, Aaron Anderson, Evan Capper, Branden Claassen, Justin Cordes, Sam DeBoer, Jessie Farley, Jason Freeseman, Tommy Gisch, Vince Gisch, Chris Grill, Ben Groen, Colin Groeneveld, Creed Harkless, Blake Harris, Josh Harris, John Hubbard, Andy Jacobson, Drew Johnson, Ethan Johnson, Rick Johnson, Justin Koenen, Tom Koenen, Shawn Krusey, Joey Larson, Kim Little, John Luhring, Bo Meester, Tyrus Meester, Caleb Meyer, Tyler Nevenhoven, Jesse Nitcher, Greg Noble, Jeremy Ohrt, Eric Ooms, Brandon Patterson, Jonah Patterson, Craig Peters, Justin Peters, Jordan Proctor, Brennan Pruisner, Tyler Reams, Kyle Reisinger, Scott Schipper, Michael Sharp, Michael Siems, John Simon, Kyle Spree, Nate Studnicka, Michael Taylor, Nick

Tjeerdsma, Curtis Tyler, Grant Ubben, Cody Vry, Stephen Walters, Jared Wildeboer, Nate Woodley, Jordan Young.

2005: Adam Aalderks, Alex Abbas, Jon Abkes, Matt Adelmund, Jacob Allspach, Billy Aukes, Sean Bellows, Zach Bradseth, Evan Capper, Jordan Choate, Branden Claassen, Justin Cordes, Sam DeBoer, Shawn Doyle, Ben Dunegan, Jessie Farley, John Gisch, Tommy Gisch, Chris Grill, James Grill, Colin Groeneveld, Creed Harkless, Josh Harris, John Hubbard, Drew Johnson, Ethan Johnson, Rick Johnson, Craig Junker, Justin Koenen, Tom Koenen, Shawn Krusey, Kyle Kwilasz, Joey Larson, Kim Little, Pat Little, Brendon Luhring, Bo Meester, Tyrus Meester, Caleb Meyer, Tyler Nevenhoven, Jesse Nitcher, Greg Noble, Jeremy Ohrt, Jonah Patterson, Justin Peters, Christian Price, Jordan Proctor, Brennan Pruisner, Kyle Reisinger, Justin Ridder, Scott Schipper, Michael Sharp, John Simon, Klayton Sprole, Nate Studnicka, Michael Taylor, Colin Tenney, Alec Thompson, Nick Tjeerdsma, Grant Ubben, Riley Ubben, Stephen Walters, Jared Wildeboer, Nate Woodley, Jordan Young, Adam Zuck.

2006: Alex Abbas, Travis Abbas, Matt Adelmund, Billy Aukes, Scott Becker, Ryan Bixby, Jim Brouwer, Evan Capper, Jordan Choate, Jimmy Clark, Sam DeBoer, Tony DeGroote, Ryan Downs, Shawn Doyle, Ben Dunegan, Andy Eggers, Jessie Farley, John Folkerts, John Gisch, Chris Grill, James Grill, Colin Groeneveld, Evan Grummitt, Matt Haege, Creed Harkless, Josh Harris, Alex Hornbuckle, John Hubbard, Jared Jansen, Drew Johnson, Ethan Johnson, Craig Junker, Justin Koenen, Alex Kreimeyer, Shawn Krusey, Kim Little, Pat Little, Brendon Luhring, John Luhring, Lane Luhring, Bryce McCauley, Alex McDaniel, Tommy Meeks, Bo Meester, Ethan Miller, Jesse Nitcher, Greg Noble, Jeremy Ohrt, Justin Peters, Christian Price, Justin Ridder, Scott Schipper, Michael Sharp, John Simon, Jordan Simon, Scott Sivola, Reece Spree, Klayton Sprole, Damion Stohr,

Michael Taylor, Colin Tenney, Alec Thompson, Stanley Tuve, Grant Ubben, Riley Ubben, Ethan Ulfers, Dave Vinton, Cody Vry, Stephen Walters, Justin Weekley, Coy Wiegmann, Michael Wiegmann, Jared Wildeboer, Jordan Young, Adam Zuck.

2007: Alex Abbas, Matt Adelmund, Mirlind Alimi, Billy Aukes, Tyler Aukes, Scott Becker, Dylan Bellows, Ryan Bixby, Colton Brouwer, Travis Brouwer, Jordan Choate, Zach Choate, Jimmy Clark, Sam Cordes, Sam DeBoer, Josh DeBower, Tony DeGroote, Michael Eastman, Andy Eggers, Jacob Everts, Chris Grill, James Grill, Austin Groeneveld, Evan Grummitt, Matt Haege, Alex Hornbuckle, John Hubbard, Drew Johnson, Alex Kreimeyer, Shawn Krusey, Pat Little, Brendon Luhring, Josh Marsh, Bryce McCauley, Joey McCracken, Alex McDaniel, Connor McDaniel, Tommy Meeks, Jacob Meester, Ethan Miller, Brett Mulder, Derek Niedert, Greg Noble, Christian Palacious, Jonah Patterson, Christian Price, Justin Ridder, Austin Ryan, Scott Schipper, Oliver Schmitz, Justin Schwark, John Simon, Jordan Simon, Scott Sivola, Damion Stohr, Colin Tenney, Alec Thompson, Sam Thompson, Zach Toben, Stanley Tuve, Riley Ubben, Ethan Ulfers, Justin Weekley, Jamey Wells, Coy Wiegmann, Michael Wiegmann, Chase Wildeboer, Jared Wildeboer, Jarod Woodley, Jordan Young.

2008: Alex Abbas, Billy Aukes, Tyler Aukes, Scott Becker, Dylan Bellows, Ryan Bixby, Colton Brouwer, Justin Bruce, Jordan Choate, Zach Choate, Jimmy Clark, Spencer Cooper, Jack Cordes, Sam Cordes, Alex Custshall, Josh DeBower, Michael Eastman, Andy Eggers, Jacob Everts, Abraham Folkerts, Stephen Graham, James Grill, Jason Grill, Austin Groeneveld, Evan Grummitt, Curry Hoff, Alex Hornbuckle, Robert Janssen, Kyle Kampman, Alex Kreimeyer, Cole Lindaman, Pat Little, Brendon Luhring, Travis Luze, Kyle Maitland, Josh Marsh, Jose Marshall, Bryce McCauley, Dayton McCauley, Joey McCracken, Alex McDaniel, Connor McDaniel, Ethan Miller, Brett Mulder, Shelton Nevenhoven, Shason Niedert, Gabe Nolte, Kyle Ooms, Christian Price, Justin Ridder, Austin Ryan, Oliver Schmitz, Justin Schwark, Brandon Simkins, Jordan Simon, Scott Sivola, Travis Slifer, Brandon Stohr, Damion Stohr, Cory Taylor, Colin Tenney, Alec Thompson, Sam Thompson, Zach Toben, Stanley Tuve, Joe Tyler, Riley Ubben, Ethan Ulfers, Jamey Wells, Matthew Wicks, Coy Wiegmann, Michael Wiegmann, Chase Wildeboer, Jarod Woodley.

COACHES

THE FOLLOWING IS A LIST OF THE COACHES WHO GOT THEIR start with Ed Thomas.

Northeast Hamilton Trojans Assistants

Ted Bieth, Mark Vermeer.

Parkersburg Crusaders Assistants

Brian Benning, Chuck Block, Brian Cassady, Bruce Crane, Eric Griffith, Steve Hester, Al Kerns, Art Oordt, Keith Schrage, Dale Stearns, Scott Striegel, Brett Thorne, Scott Wagner, Jon Wiegmann.

Aplington-Parkersburg Falcons Assistants

Todd Carr, Casey Christensen, Tim Cuvelier, Justin Davies, Dusty DeVries, Jay DeVries, Clint Dohlman, Greg Fisher, Travis Foster, Cory Groeneveld, Jason Halverson, Ryan Halverson, Mark Haren, Scott Heitland, Steve Hester, Mark Hubbard, Levi Hunerdosse, Michael Irvin, Matt Jacobson, Brad Jones, Jeff Juhl, Al Kerns, Jason Key, Matt Kingsbury, Brad Knight, Brett Kramer, Dustin Larson, Justin Manifold, Dave McGill, Pat Rowan, Bernie Sohm, Todd Thomas, Cody Ubben, Milt Ulfers, Heath Walton, Jon Wiegmann, Kelly Williamson.

ACKNOWLEDGMENTS

FOR COACH THOMAS, EVERY GAME WAS ALWAYS ABOUT THE team. "The only way we win is for us all to work together," he preached. Although I never played for Coach Thomas, his words echoed in my ears as I worked on this book. It was truly a team effort.

First and foremost, I would like to thank Jan, Aaron, and Todd for entrusting Ed's story to me. You shared so much of him with me that I feel like I knew him. I appreciate your opening your lives up in such a personal way during our interviews, as well as your patience with me as I flooded your in-boxes with questions day after day. No one should ever have to live through the nightmare the three of you endured, yet you did so with such grace and forgiveness that through you an act of evil has become a force for good. Thank you for allowing me to play a small role in spreading this message. Thank you as well to Ellie and Candice for sharing your experiences with me through Tony Wilson for this book.

Speaking of Tony, this book would never have happened without you. Thank you for taking the lead in finding a way to tell Coach Thomas's story. I appreciate your choosing me as the writer for the book, as well as the way in which you gladly took on the role of my "research assistant." The stack of DVDs you gave me of Ed's speeches and the team videos and news coverage of both Parkersburg tragedies were vital to telling this story. I also appreciate all of the interviews you conducted and your constant encouragement during the writing process.

A special word of thanks to Ed's sisters, Susan Reynolds, Connie Flaherty, Teresa Morrison, and his brother, Greg, for taking time to share with me stories of life in the Thomas household when Ed was a child. I cannot fathom the hurt the four of you carry from the loss of your brother. Thank you for helping me understand who he truly was.

The stories within this book came from hours of interviews with Ed's family, friends, players, and the people of Parkersburg, Iowa. Thank you to Chris Luhring, who gave me many of the stories in chapters 3, 16, and 17. Chris also provided insight into the long and difficult road to passing the Ed Thomas Bill. Ron Westerman told me invaluable stories about the cleanup and rebuilding of the football field. Thank you, Ron, for making time for me on Thanksgiving weekend. Thank you to school superintendent Jon Thompson and high school principal Dave Meyers, who contributed stories about the rebuilding process. The 2008 A-P Falcon players Coy Wiegmann, Alec Thompson, and Michael Wiegmann showed me the summer of rebuilding from the team's perspective and made Coach's final season come alive to me. Thank you, guys, for answering my random texts and e-mails in such a timely manner. Former Falcon Rusty Eddy gave me insight into the character of Coach and the impact he had on his players in a very personal way. Thank you, Rusty, for sharing your story with me through Tony Wilson. Thank you as well to Aaron Kampman, Casey Wiegmann, Brad Meester, and Jared DeVries for sharing your experiences with Coach Thomas. Coach Tom Wilson shared the stories about his friend that became chapter 7; while Coach Scott Heitland's stories of Ed's last day became chapter 15. Thank you to both men. I also deeply appreciate Tom Teeple and his wife, Sue, for eagerly opening up and sharing so many stories about Ed. Although I did not use most of these, you helped me come to know Ed. The two of you knew him longer than anyone outside of his family. And thank you to Dave and Joan Becker for sharing their stories about Coach.

Others who were interviewed for this book and the film project by the same name include Pastor Ron Barlett, Scott Becker, Neil and Staci Brumgaard, Rick Coleman, Tim and Shelli Cuvelier, Reid Forgrave, Virgil Goodrich, Jim and Grace Graves, Mark Hubbard, Stub Huisman, Dennis Ihde, Jeff Jacobson, Everett Jansen, Al and Deb Kerns, Orlyn and Wendy Marks, Daryl Myers, Emma Peterson, Mary Rice, Tim and Kim Schnell, Craig Schrage, Jon Wiegmann, Kelly Williamson, and Pastor Brad Zinnecker.

As with any team, some of the most vital members work behind the scenes. Thank you, Lee Hough, for all you do. We make a great team. I thank God for you. I also want to thank my transcriptionist extraordinaire, Sarah Tabb. Thank you as well to the team at Zondervan. Finally, thank you to the best editor in the world, Liz Heaney.